THE HUNTING & FISHING LIBRARY®

ADVANCED WHITETAIL HUNTING

By Ron Spomer and Gary Clancy

RON SPOMER'S 20-year tenure as a hunting writer and photographer is exceeded only by his 30-year career as a whitetail deer hunter. Starting at age 14 in South Dakota, Ron has hunted whitetails in nine states with rifle, bow and muzzleloader. His articles and photographs have appeared in many books and more than 90 magazines.

GARY CLANCY has hunted deer across North America with rifle, shotgun, muzzleloader, pistol and bow. A full-time free-lance outdoor writer, Gary's articles and photos appear regularly in regional and national magazines. He coauthored *White-Tailed Deer* for The Hunting & Fishing Library.

COWLES
Creative Publishing, Inc.

President/COO: Nino Tarantino
Executive V.P./Editor-in-Chief: William B. Jones

ADVANCED WHITETAIL HUNTING
By Ron Spomer and Gary Clancy

Executive Editor, Outdoor Products Group: Don Oster
Contributing Writer and Book Development Leader: David Maas
Senior Editor: Bryan Trandem
Technical Advisor: Tom Carpenter
Copy Editor: Janice Cauley
Project Manager: Denise Bornhausen
Senior Art Director: Dave Schelitzche
Senior Desktop Publishing Specialist: Joe Fahey
Desktop Publishing Specialist: Laurie Kristensen
Director of Photography: Mike Parker
Studio Manager: Marcia Chambers
Principal Photographer: William Lindner
Staff Photographers: Mike Hehner, Rebecca Schmitt
Photo Assistants: Thomas Heck, Dave Tieszen
Photo Editor: Anne Price
V.P. Development Planning and Production: Jim Bindas
Production Manager: Stasia Dorn
Production Staff: Laura Hokkanen, Tom Hoops, Troy Johnson, Jeannette Moss, Mike Schauer
Electronic Illustrations: Earl Slack
Cover Photo: Bill Kinney

Contributing Photographers: Charles J. Alsheimer, Mike Biggs, Denver Bryan, Gary Clancy, Jeanne Drake, The Green Agency, Donald M. Jones, Bill Kinney, Lance Krueger, Bill Lea, Steve Maas, Bill Marchel, Ted Rose, Ron Spomer

Consulting Individuals, Agencies and Manufacturers: ALS Enterprises/Scent Lok – Jim Hill, Greg Sesselmann; Atsko/Sno-Seal Inc. – Kurt Von Besser; Berkley Inc. – Barry Day; Jim Borg; Bowhunter Magazine – Dave Canfield, M. R. James; Mel Dutton; James Valley Scents – John Collins; Knight & Hale Game Calls – David Hale, Harold Knight; Don Laubach; Lohman Mfg. Company, Inc. – Brad Harris; Minnesota Department of Natural Resources – Jay McAninch; Modern Muzzleloading Inc. – Toby Bridges; Montana Critter Co. – Harry Brunett; Lee and Lonnie Murphy; Northern Sun

Outdoor Group, Inc./Backland – Scott Anderson; John Oster; John J. Ozoga; Primos, Inc. – Will Primos; Gary Sefton; South Dakota Dept. of Tourism – Mark Kayser; Southwest Missouri State University – Dr. Lynn Robbins, Grant Woods; Spartan Realtree – Bill Jordan; Mike Sullivan; Texas Parks and Wildlife Department – Bryan Richards; Louis J. Verme; Larry Weishuhn; Wellington Outdoors – Terry Rohm; Curt Wells; West Virginia University – Dr. David Samuel; Woods Wise Products – Jerry Peterson; Jim Zumbo

Contributing Manufacturers: ASAT Camouflage; Beman Archery Corp.; Browning – Paul Thompson; Cabela's, Inc. – Tony Dolle, Stephanie Geiger; Carry-Lite Decoys – Bob Kufahl; Haas Outdoors Inc. – Toxey Haas; Mountaineer Archery – Pat Nealis; Muzzy Products Corp.; Osmic Research Company/Dr. Juice; Redishot – Bill Mocca; Scrape Juice Hunting Products; Screaming Eagle, Inc. – Lad Brunner; Sport-Flex, Inc./Feather Flex Decoys – Dave Berkley; Summit Specialties, Inc. – Brian Tommerdahl; Winchester Division/Olin Corp. – Mike Jordan

Contributing Individuals and Agencies: Baker's Ribs – Al Killion; Paul Bernard; Bill Bornhausen; Burger Brothers – Dave Johnston; Bob Fleskes; Chris and Greg Gulden; Kevin Howard; Bob Knoph; Terry Krahn; Jay Mahs; Markhurd Photogrammetric Engineers – Lon Juergens; Ray McIntyre; Greg Miller; Minnesota Department of Natural Resources – Paul Rice; Moon Valley Shooting Range; Jim Moynagh; Corky Richardson; Mike Sheehan; Jim Shockey; Terry Stone; Wayne Tieszen; Pat and Tom Wagamon; Mike Wieck

Printed on American paper by: R. R. Donnelley & Sons Co.
00 99 98 97 / 5 4 3 2 1

Library of Congress
Cataloging-in-Publication Data

Spomer, Ronald Lee.
Advanced whitetail hunting / Ronald Lee Spomer, Gary Clancy.
p. cm.
Incudes index.
ISBN 0-86573-055-5
1. White-tailed deer hunting. I. Clancy, Gary. II. Title.
SK301.S7 1996   96-1165
799.2'77357--dc20

Contents

Introduction

Hunting whitetails is more than a seasonal diversion for hundreds of thousands of serious deer hunters. In late winter, these dedicated outdoorsmen watch whitetail videos, search for shed antlers and attend hunting shows. In spring and summer, they tune bows and rifles, study scientific research, and make scouting pilgrimages into the field. And from fall through midwinter, congregations of hunters pursue North America's most abundant, most adaptable and most elusive deer – the whitetail.

And why not? For centuries before Europeans arrived in North America, native hunters harvested millions of whitetails each year. Today's whitetail population stands at more than 20 million after declining to a low of a few hundred thousand in the early 1900s. As the world shrinks and technology advances, whitetails remain our connection to wilderness, to a slower time and a more natural way of life.

We have written *Advanced Whitetail Hunting* to provide today's experienced deer hunter with the latest tactics for outwitting wary bucks – those heavily antlered, mature animals that have learned to outflank and outmaneuver casual hunters.

In the first section, "Techniques of the Experts," some of North America's most successful trophy buck hunters outline their secrets for locating and hunting those super bucks. Every effective whitetail hunting strategy is covered – from good, old-fashioned still-hunting to the modern techniques of calling, rattling and decoying. The section starts off with a chapter on scouting, the essential first step for anyone who seeks a mature, experienced deer. The diligent scout who finds his buck and learns its territory and habits before hunting season opens has a huge advantage over other hunters.

"Special Situations" describes unique hunting opportunities in unusual places, such as vast cornfields and cattail sloughs. In the past, virtually no one hunted these areas – which may be the reason they harbor so many of today's biggest bucks. Scrape-hunting, often recommended but seldom understood, is thoroughly explained in light of the latest scientific research and the observations of expert hunters. We've devoted an entire chapter to the subject of hunting bedding areas, because the subject is so difficult. One false move here, and the game's over.

"Fooling the Whitetail's Nose" examines the latest techniques and products used to stymie the whitetail's powerful sense of smell. First, you'll learn a detailed strategy that makes it possible to virtually eliminate human odor. Then, we'll show you how to create the ultimate illusion, luring bucks by using natural whitetail scents in conjunction with rattling, calling and decoying.

Finally, "For Trophies Only" is a graduate course for hunters seeking record-book bucks. First, you'll learn how to distinguish between true trophies and second-best bucks, using quick and accurate field-judging techniques. With a little practice, you'll be able to instantly identify monsters with potential for the Pope and Young or Boone and Crockett record books. And because hunting mature deer requires a knowledge of trophy buck behavior, we've included a bonus chapter on "Hunting Mature Bucks" to help you outwit them.

Unique among deer hunting books, *Advanced Whitetail Hunting* is filled with detailed illustrations, charts, maps – and hundreds of color photos showing every aspect of whitetail hunting, from using aerial photos to scout for whitetail habitat, to luring a trophy buck with doe-in-estrus scent. This is one book in which you'll learn as much from the photos and illustrations as you do from the text.

We've taken a different approach with the text as well. Many whitetail hunting books feature a detailed account by a single hunter; the author may be an expert in his neck of the woods, but his information may not apply to your area. For this book, we instead interviewed experts from North and South, East and West to compile this comprehensive guide for all readers. Whether you hunt north woods, eastern hardwoods, midwest farmland, southern pine plantations, swamps, plains, cattail sloughs, river valleys or western mountains, *Advanced Whitetail Hunting* has you covered. If you aren't already a whitetail expert, you'll be well on your way after studying this book. Happy hunting.

— Ron Spomer & Gary Clancy

Techniques of
the Experts

Scouting

All successful trophy whitetail hunters – and we're talking about the select few who seem to tag huge bucks year after year – have one skill in common: the ability to scout. An ordinary, run-of-the-mill hunter may have the best equipment, might be an accomplished marksman and can be very adept at the standard techniques of stand-hunting and still-hunting. But the ability to scout effectively is the one skill that separates expert hunters from the legions of mediocre hunters who thrash about the countryside each season, hoping to stumble upon a buck to shoot.

Expert hunters know that accurate, thorough scouting is the key to taking big bucks. Whether you hunt in the North, South, East or West, on popular public land or a private sanctuary, your odds for success improve when you know the lay of the land and understand how whitetails behave in that territory.

Despite this simple truth, we've known many hunters who would rather hike a bog in leaky boots than spend their off-season weekends scouting for whitetails. If

you fall into this category, motivate yourself by remembering a few of the days when you spent eight or ten cold, motionless hours on stand in damp woods without even a glimpse of a deer.

You may be surprised at some of the scouting techniques used by expert whitetail hunters. Good old-fashioned legwork plays a part, of course, especially when you are hiking known whitetail habitat to plan strategy for the upcoming hunt. But a good whitetail

Map Types

Topographical maps can be ordered from:
USGS Information Services,
P.O. Box 25286, Denver, CO 80225.
Phone 1-800-USA-MAPS

Aerial photos can be ordered from:
Aerial Photography Field Office, User Services,
P.O. Box 30010, Salt Lake City, UT 84130.
Phone (801) 975-3503

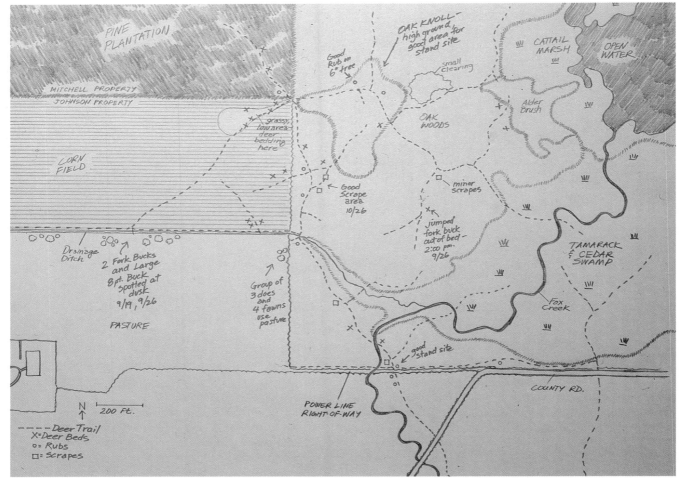

Hand-drawn map

![Plat book map]

Plat book

Aerial photo taken from a rented plane

scout must also have the ability to interpret academic research, and to read technical maps and aerial photos. And you must be outgoing and personable enough to meet strangers and coax them into revealing what they know about local whitetail action.

And throughout the scouting process, you'll need a solid understanding of four important aspects of whitetail behavior: what deer eat, where they bed, how they move through habitat and how they act during the breeding season.

Identifying Likely Deer Habitat

Begin your research by buying a map of the county you want to hunt and getting a local phone book. We strongly recommend you buy a plat book (above) at the county courthouse. Costing $10 to $25, the plat book identifies the ownership and boundaries of each piece of property.

Next, try to obtain aerial photos or topographical maps of the area you want to hunt. Aerial photos are highly detailed, making it possible to identify likely whitetail habitat. Costing as much as $35 each, aerial photos may be available from your local Agricultural Stabilization and Conservation Service office (ASCS); or you can order them directly from the Aerial Photography Field Office (opposite page). To get the right photos, you'll need to provide the

legal description of the property, as listed in your plat book, and label the property on a county road map.

Topographical maps are especially useful in hilly country. Costing about $5 each, these charts are not as detailed as aerial photos, but they do show elevation as well as major features that influence deer movement – wooded and open areas, streams and lakes, marshes and agricultural areas, roads, power lines, railway lines and other natural and man-made features. Topographical maps are sold in many sporting goods stores, or can be ordered from the U.S. Geological Survey (opposite page). You'll need a state index to determine which maps cover your hunting area. The most useful maps have a scale of 1:24,000 and cover about 50 square miles.

If aerial photos or topographical maps are unavailable, you can also draw your own map by hand (opposite page), filling in details while exploring the area by vehicle and on foot. Where practical, charter a small plane for an invaluable bird's-eye view of your potential hunting area (above). Renting a plane can cost $100 or more per hour, but splitting this cost with another hunter or two makes the expense well worthwhile. An hour in the air can show you more than a week spent hiking on foot. From a high altitude, you can map and photograph the major features of the terrain, and at lower altitudes you'll be able to pinpoint deer trails, bedding areas and feeding fields – especially if the ground is covered with snow. If you fly at dawn or dusk, you may spot deer in the open.

TRAVEL CORRIDORS, or *funnels,* are narrow bottlenecks formed where open fields, lakes, rivers or other obstacles force deer into a narrow area of cover.

Now that you have maps and/or aerial photos in hand, spread them out on your kitchen table and examine them, keeping in mind the ways whitetails use this habitat. Although you'll eventually need to explore the terrain on foot, you can identify many likely locations simply by studying your maps and photos closely.

Start by looking for probable feeding areas. Agricultural crop fields are prime whitetail feeding grounds, but food preferences vary according to season. Call wildlife management and agricultural extension offices to learn which crops whitetails favor. In much of North America, whitetails eat soybeans in early fall, alfalfa and green wheat from late summer to late fall, and corn from late fall through winter.

In fall, whitetails also feed on acorns in oak forests, but identifying these feeding sites is more difficult because deer prefer different types of acorns in different regions. In much of the Midwest, for example, deer will seek out the acorns from a single white oak isolated in a forest of red oaks. Consult state game biologists or university researchers to learn which type of acorns the local deer prefer, and when these trees drop their acorns. Identifying oak species requires some field work in late summer. Use binoculars to identify trees from a distance, and inspect the upper branches for large quantities of acorns. Later, when heavily laden trees begin to drop their acorns, you'll almost certainly find deer feeding below them.

In forested areas, commercial clear-cut logging creates grassy browsing areas that may be a prime whitetail food source if agricultural crops and acorns are not available. In the South, clear-cuts develop browsing vegetation almost immediately after the trees are harvested, but, in the North, it takes a season or two before deer begin to feed in these areas.

Next, examine your maps and photos for bedding sites. Thickets, second-growth brush, marshes and swamps near feeding areas are likely whitetail bedding locations.

Finally, try to identify probable deer travel routes. This is mostly a matter of pinpointing the obvious paths from feeding grounds to bedding sites. Examine your maps and photos, looking for areas where large lakes, major highways, steep cliffs, timbered bottlenecks or human development force deer into narrow travel lanes between feeding and bedding areas. We've always found good hunting along these pathways.

Scouting in the Field

Now it's time to hit the field and enter the whitetail's world on foot. For obvious reasons, scouting done just before the hunting season provides the most timely and reliable information, but you must be careful not to alert deer and disrupt their normal behavior patterns. Use binoculars to check sign

RUBS made by bucks raking their antlers on trees, are often found along paths between bedding and feeding areas. On routes used repeatedly by bucks, many rubs dot the trail, forming *rub lines*.

RUNNING TRACKS leading to dense, isolated cover often identify escape routes used by deer once hunting pressure gets heavy. Running tracks have side-by-side hind prints ahead of the front prints.

whenever possible, and avoid contaminating any more habitat than is absolutely necessary. Wear camouflage, and scout on a rainy or windy day, when deer are less likely to smell or hear you. If you are scouting private land, use your plat book and telephone directory to identify landowners, then contact them to secure permission to scout and hunt on their property. Many landowners will grant permission to a hunter who approaches them tactfully (p. 121).

Once in the field, you'll be looking for whitetail sign that confirms what you suspected from studying your maps and photos. You're hoping to spot deer sign that identifies active feeding and bedding sites and the pathways leading between these areas. A buck's bedroom will have a few large beds, while a doe and fawn bedroom will have numerous beds of varying sizes.

As you explore, update your maps to pinpoint promising locations. With a hand-held global positioning system, or *GPS* (right), which operates by using signals from orbital satellites, you

can lock in the precise coordinates for these locations and easily find them later.

When scouting in fall, you'll find it easy to identify rutting sign – the most important clue if you're looking to tag a trophy buck. Look for rubs, scrapes and areas of torn-up ground where bucks have been battling. These clues tell you where bucks have been and where they're likely to show up in the near future.

Although most in-the-field scouting is done just before the hunting season, there is plenty of motivation to hike the terrain at other times of the year. Some scouting is essential during the hunt itself, particularly for bowhunters who enjoy a season of three months or more. Your quarry may well change his bedding and feeding sites in response to normal seasonal changes in vegetation, or because of hunting pressure.

When hunters in large numbers begin to invade whitetail habitat during hunting season, deer may be pressured into using routes they don't normally travel, leading to temporary bedding sites in impenetrable, isolated cover. If you see running deer tracks (above) already leading into these areas, it may be too late; when a buck has made his getaway and found seclusion, he might not show himself in daylight for the remainder of the season. But mark your maps and make plans to ambush deer along these escape routes next season.

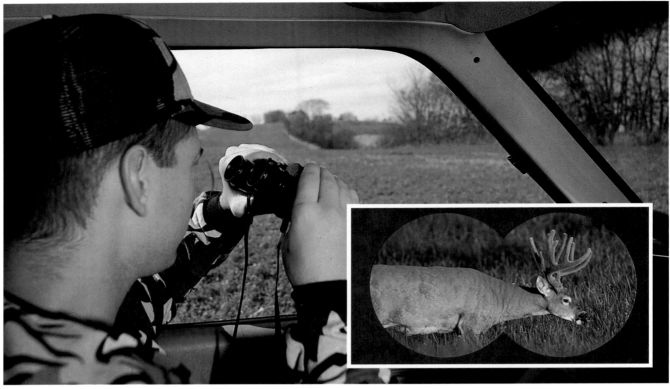

IN LATE SUMMER, glassing is the best way to spot a big buck. Slowly drive country roads at dusk, glassing feed fields from your car or truck. Stay in your vehicle to avoid spooking deer.

IN WINTER, you can identify bedding areas by the melted depressions in the snow and the presence of droppings.

IN EARLY SPRING, look for shed antlers, which indicate the quality of surviving bucks in the area.

Some hunters scout for these in-season behavior changes while they are still-hunting, but you'll probably do better if you pick one day to concentrate fully on interpreting sign, then use another day to actually hunt the new location.

Although few hunters do it, scouting just after a hunting season can be revealing. At this time you can crash into those dense, isolated bedding areas to find out if they really were being used by whitetails. Explore all the places you wondered about during the season – the deer you roust will have all year to get over their fright, and you may discover promising rub lines, beds and funnels that will be productive next year.

In early spring before green-up, make a point of getting out in the field again. Last fall's rubs, scrapes and trails still show clearly. Popular bedding areas are marked with concentrated whitetail droppings, and shed antlers tell you the size of surviving bucks.

By late summer, bucks have grown new antlers and become accustomed to road traffic. This is the perfect time to use binoculars or a spotting scope to glass feed fields at dawn and dusk. You might not see every buck in the area, but you'll get to know quite a few. The deer may switch patterns within a few weeks, but at least you'll know their general territory. To catch sight of super-wary nocturnal bucks, try spotlighting, if the technique is legal in your area. But be considerate – no property owner appreciates bright lights shining across his house and yard.

Scouting whitetails is a time-consuming business that requires year-round dedication. But making yourself a skilled whitetail scout virtually guarantees that your next hunting season will be productive. It's the single best way to become the kind of outdoorsman other hunters admire and turn to when they need advice.

Cafe Deer Spy

It's often easier to find a monster buck with your ears than with your eyes and legs. In addition to scouting woods and fields, hang out at popular cafes and coffee shops.

Local residents tend to notice exceptionally big deer, and when they see one, they like to talk about it. "Harold almost hit a big buck on the Lake Road yesterday," one farmer might be overheard saying in a small town cafe. "Said it looked like an elk." Prick up your ears when you overhear this kind of conversation, and, if necessary, tell a big buck story of your own to aim the conversation in the right direction.

Don't be bashful. Talk about bucks at the gas station, the barber shop and the farmers' co-op. Find an excuse to stop by every store and tavern, and when you do, talk about big deer. People will soon know you as the "deer fanatic," and every big buck sighting will eventually reach you.

Many rumors are just that, of course. And one person's "monster buck" is another's average eight-pointer. Nevertheless, follow each rumor to determine its validity. If you like what you hear, go to each site as soon as possible and ask permission to scout the area. The landowner may well know the buck's habits, saving you hours of time.

Still-Hunting

Few techniques bring you closer to the primal satisfaction of the hunting experience than still-hunting. This method of moving at a slow prowl with senses on full alert, periodically freezing to ambush unsuspecting prey, is perhaps the oldest and most successful hunting strategy in the books. Mountain lions do it. Native Americans armed with wooden bows and stone broadheads practiced it to perfection. Early American woodsmen and mountain men employed the technique, and there's no reason why 20th-century hunters can't still-hunt. And many do just that; thousands of tuned-in hunters successfully still-hunt each year.

Many hunters think of still-hunting as a mystical, intuitive art beyond their skills, but this is just nonsense. Still-hunting does require patience, discipline and control, but like any technique, it can be learned. All it takes is a positive attitude, confidence and attention to details. And you'll find that the rewards are immense.

To understand still-hunting, think of it as mobile stand-hunting. The objectives are the same – to spot a buck within range and shoot it before it detects you. The only difference is that the still-hunter can cover a lot more territory because he moves his stand from time to time. And as he moves, every sense is alive and on full alert, concentrating on sights, sounds and even scents. An expert still-hunter knows which way the breeze is blowing, whether thermals are rising or sinking, whether to skirt a thicket or slip through it.

Still-Hunting Basics

Unlike many hunting methods, which are passive, still-hunting is an active strategy that allows you to react to what you see. A still-hunter who spots a buck crossing a field or meadow hundreds of yards away can move to intercept it, while the stand-hunter must helplessly watch it move out of sight. Because still-hunting puts a premium on stealth, it's a good technique if you're hunting alone.

Still-hunting also is a perfect way to hunt new areas. As you move, you'll discover rub lines, scrapes and beds that give you valuable clues about deer behavior in the area – information you can use to great advantage during future hunts.

Still-hunting is best suited for gun hunters, since they can shoot effectively at much greater distances than bowhunters. The technique works best in an area populated with lots of deer, in semi-open to open cover with a soft, quiet ground surface. In this habitat, you can move silently and see far enough to spot deer before they sense you.

Still-hunting also works well in hilly terrain where you can sneak over ridges and spot unsuspecting deer at short range. Feeding sites – such as orchards, oak woods, second-growth woods and the edges of crop fields – are ideal for still-hunting, because they draw large numbers of deer. Browsing whitetails focused on feeding are relaxed and easier to approach than bedded deer.

Terrain with numerous trails leading from feeding to bedding sites are also excellent places to still-hunt. The best trails will be dotted with rubs and scrapes.

Don't try to still-hunt over ground covered with dry leaves or crunchy snow, conditions that make it

impossible to move silently. And don't still-hunt where dense brush makes it difficult to see more than 30 to 40 yards; under these conditions, deer will almost always sense you before you see them.

As you might guess, the best season to still-hunt is just before and during the rut, when bucks are on their feet throughout the day, scraping, rubbing, scent-marking limbs and chasing females. At other times of the year, still-hunting can be successful in the morning and late afternoon, when deer are moving between feeding and bedding areas, but during the daylight hours, when whitetails are bedded and watchful, still-hunting is a poor choice.

Many hunters make the common mistake of always stand-hunting the prime morning and afternoon hours, and still-hunting only during the slow midday period. Don't make this error. Unless you have a

really hot stand site and know exactly where deer are feeding, bedding or traveling, your chances for intercepting a buck are often best if you actively still-hunt the best hours – early morning and late afternoon.

As a rule, whatever the weather or habitat, if you can see farther than your sound carries, you have the green light for still-hunting. Dry, calm weather is always the poorest for still-hunting, since the vegetation is noisy and sound carries well. Stay motionless and stand-hunt on those days. But still-hunting should be your choice when there's a steady breeze or light rain to cover noises. And when rain, snow or melting frost wets the ground, your footsteps will be muffled, allowing you to move like fog over the ground. In hilly habitat, shaded north slopes remain moist and quiet longer than south slopes, which are dried quickly by the sun.

COVER UP your sound when crossing a noisy area, like ground covered with dry leaves, by waiting for the noise of a passing truck or a strong wind.

SIT COMFORTABLY at any location by carrying a portable chair made of fleece. The best models are carried on your back (left) and allow you to sit at a comfortable height (right).

REMOVE shotgun and rifle slings when still-hunting; these straps could catch on brush and make noise.

FOOL deer after you break a branch by using a turkey or squirrel call (inset). Whitetails are at ease around these animals and will probably ignore the disturbance.

CLEAR your path for quiet passage by carefully cutting away brush with small, sharp pruning shears.

DETECT wind direction and rising and falling thermals by squeezing unscented powder into the air.

STILL-HUNT downhill in the late morning (above) and uphill in the late afternoon, because thermals rise in the late morning as the air heats up and descend in the evening as the air cools down.

How to Still-Hunt

Clothes make the still-hunter. Dress head to toe in soft, quiet materials like wool, brushed cotton or fleece. Wear clothes that keep you warm, dry and comfortable. You'll be moving at a snail's pace, so dress as if you were going to sit on stand all day. It's impossible to concentrate on effective, slow still-hunting when you're shivering.

Gun hunters should wear blaze-orange camouflage (where legal) to break up their outline; bowhunters, a camo pattern that blends with the ground cover. All hunters need to camouflage their face and hands, which draw attention because they are most often in motion.

Your hat should keep the sun out of your eyes, but it shouldn't have such a wide brim that it catches on branches. Soft-soled boots will cushion and muffle your footsteps. Some dedicated still-hunters wear thin-soled moccasins or rubber-bottomed pacs so they can detect debris beneath their feet and ease up when they feel a stick about to break.

Before you set foot in the field, pump up your confidence. If you believe you'll be successful, you probably will be. Hunt like a true predator, fully alert, completely focused. You're not a naturalist out for a stroll; you're a cat stalking dinner.

It's easiest to maintain such confidence if you're hunting good country, an area crawling with bucks. If you're hunting new territory, begin where the sign suggests deer are present – look for trails, scrapes, droppings, rubs and beds. If you don't see such sign, quickly move on. Don't waste time in unproductive areas, but when you reach a spot with good sign, still-hunt with maximum stealth, as if a buck is behind the next tree.

Continually read the breeze. If you feel cold air descending, hunt uphill; hunt downhill if warm air is rising. Don't automatically assume that air rises in the morning and falls in the evening. In late autumn, even on sunny days, it may take a few hours before the ground heats up enough to create uprising thermals. In late afternoon, when cooling, sinking air normally carries your scent downhill, a warm weather front moving in can send air rising instead.

Regardless of wind conditions, pay close attention to controlling and masking your odor (p. 104). No matter how slowly you move and how well you hide, if a deer smells you, the game is over. Whenever possible, put the rising or setting sun at your back as you still-hunt. Deer looking into intense sunlight will have a difficult time spotting you.

Before you start walking, scan the terrain ahead and to both sides, looking first for motion, then for any shape or color that might be a deer – the glint of an eye or antler; the horizontal dark line of a back or white line of a belly; the curve of a rump; the flick of an ear or tail. The successful still-hunter is the one who can identify deer from small glimpses through grass or brush. Use binoculars if you need to, but raise and lower them slowly.

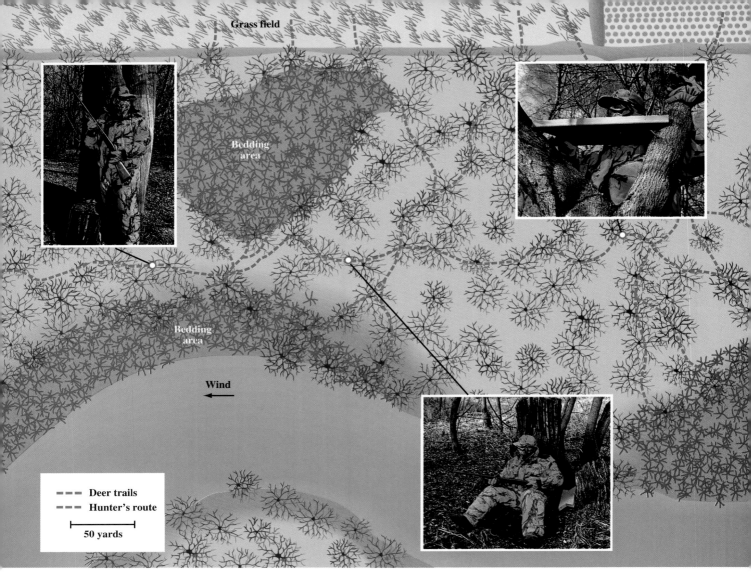

Grass field

Bedding area

Bedding area

Wind

- - - Deer trails
- - - Hunter's route

50 yards

PLAN your still-hunt so you'll pass through areas known to contain deer, and choose several stand sites with sufficient cover to hide your presence. In the example shown above, the hunter's first stand site was against a wide tree, which he used to break up his outline. After an hour or so, he moved to the next site, where he sat on the ground, disguising his profile by leaning

Next, stretch your search to the edge of your view. Whether 50 yards away in brush or 300 yards on prairie, this area is where most of your critical sightings will be. When you're satisfied nothing is near, move slowly forward just far enough to open a fresh view. In heavy woods this might be only a step or two until you can see around trees. In farm country or prairie, you might move several hundred yards. The thicker the cover, the slower your progress. Remember, you're stand-hunting on the move: the less you walk, the more you'll see.

Try to avoid making unnatural sounds, like the noises made by zippers, snaps, and metal clinking against metal; but don't worry if you rustle some leaves, snap a small twig or make a few other natural noises. Just don't establish a steady walking cadence. If you do, your noise will sound unnatural. If you need to move ahead quickly, perhaps to follow a buck glimpsed

moving over a rise, move in spurts like a squirrel or turkey, stopping every so often to watch and listen. If you kick a rock or make some other major commotion, wait about 5 minutes for things to calm down before moving again. Deer have relatively short memories; if they don't confirm a sound with sight or scent, they'll resume normal behavior in a few minutes.

Select your route to avoid terrain with major clearings and noisy debris. If you must move to the far side of a clearing, skirt it along the edge, keeping inside cover. Disguise your movement by skirting pockets of heavy cover and choosing a route where you won't be silhouetted against the sky – along a bank, fenceline or old road cut, down an erosion ditch or along the side of a hill. As you progress, continue scanning from side to side, concentrating on new territory as it appears. Move slowly, so you'll

Standing corn

Bedding area

Bedding area

against a tall stump. About 2 hours later, he moved to the next site, where he took up an elevated stand by placing a crotch board in the "Y" of a tree. An hour later, the hunter took a new stand at the base of a fallen tree, hiding in its uplifted root system. For his final stand of the day, the hunter slipped in between three trees that gave him cover from several directions.

be able to freeze in an instant. If you identify a deer's back over a rise of ground, you may have only a split second before it lifts its head and spots you. If you have frozen in place, the deer will probably overlook you, twitch its tail and return to foraging.

Whitetails are expert at spotting movement, but rather poor at identifying stationary objects. That's why it's so important to move slowly while still-hunting. Thousands of motionless hunters have watched in amazement as deer wandered within arm's length, as though the hunter were no more dangerous than a stump. But wiggle a finger or turn your head, and those deer instantly recognize a predator.

If you enter an area with numerous big rubs and fresh scrapes, slow down to a barely perceptible creep, taking tiny steps to maintain your balance. Lift each foot slowly and place it carefully, ball first,

feeling the ground before placing weight on it. Keep your head up, eyes watching, gun or bow ready. Listen for snapping twigs, footsteps and the sounds of a buck rubbing his antlers on a tree. At your first opportunity, take up a nearby stand location. Sit comfortably against a trunk or bush to break your outline, and wait silently. If no deer appear in a few hours, move your stand location to a new area.

Still-hunting requires a hunter who is willing to shrug off the fast-paced human schedule and tune in to the rhythms of nature. Dial your senses to their maximum settings, pay attention to your surroundings, heed your intuition, and hunt with confidence that you'll see your buck before it sees you. If you're up to the challenge, still-hunting can be the most rewarding of all hunting techniques.

Stand-Hunting

According to surveys, more deer are taken by hunters on stand than by all other methods combined. The reasons are obvious: a moving predator makes noise and is easily seen, while a motionless one makes no noise and is virtually invisible to whitetails.

Stand-hunting is, quite simply, *the* bread-and-butter technique, for archers and gun hunters alike. Those who master it are some of the most successful trophy-buck hunters in North America. When the ground is too noisy for still-hunting, when thick fog makes it impossible to glass and stalk, or when you're alone without companions to drive deer, stand-hunting is hard to beat.

Stand-Hunting Basics

Stand-hunting is one of the few techniques that works in all terrain and habitats, and any time of year. But you can use it to best advantage during the rut, when bucks are moving throughout the day, searching for romance.

Naturally, you can't just pull up a stump anywhere and expect a trophy buck to wander past. In an ideal scenario – an area with little or no hunting pressure – you'll scout thoroughly, observe your buck and pattern his movements, then set your ambush based on his schedule. But in the real world, how you stand-hunt depends mostly on the intensity of hunting pressure in the area. One other person afield can put a buck off its pattern; a small army of hunters will disrupt his schedule in a major way.

Where hunting pressure is intense (p. 92), bucks often choose the meanest, wettest, thickest chunk of brushy real estate in which to hide. Because this is the last place most hunters penetrate, it's the first place bucks go to escape – and exactly the place you want your stand. Position yourself either deep inside the cover or on obvious trails and funnels at the edge.

Ordinary coverts that are off-limits to most hunters can be equally good spots. Forty acres of wooded private land, closed to all hunters (except you) and surrounded by heavily hunted property, can be paradise. Anyplace that offers a quiet refuge during the season can become a big-buck holding cell – even small weed patches bordering rural backyards.

Under moderate hunting pressure, deer may alter their normal daily patterns but won't abandon them entirely. They generally use the same feeding and bedding sites, but travel to and from them using routes that lie in heavy cover. They won't enter clearings until it is nearly dark. Under these conditions, position yourself in one of these protected travel corridors, or inside cover just adjacent to a feeding field. If you're dead set on pursuing a trophy buck, the best stand site will be close to the buck's bedding area. Mature bucks are almost always the first to enter and last to leave bed sites, so the closer your stand, the better your chances.

Should you be one of the lucky few who has exclusive permission to hunt where others can't, rejoice. Deer will do what they normally do – feed, scrape, rub and fight – all during legal shooting hours. Deer that experience no hunting pressure are not nocturnal by nature, but *crepuscular*, meaning they are most active at dawn and dusk. Under these conditions, the best hunting will be near feeding sites, such as small orchards, oak ridges and alfalfa fields. During the rut, bucks will use these feeding sites either to eat or to find females. Place your stand where deer are most likely to enter or exit the area.

Elevated Stands

For many hunters, and certainly the vast majority of bowhunters, stand-hunting means getting above deer by using some type of elevated stand. When placed 15 feet or more off the ground, an elevated stand lets you view considerable terrain while reducing the chances of being detected by deer.

There are many types of elevated stands, and your choice depends primarily on habitat and on your weapon. For instance, if you're rifle hunting in an open area with low-growing brush and no large trees, where your shots will be 100 to 250 yards long, a tripod stand with gun supports is a good choice. However, if you are bowhunting in an oak forest, your shots will be close, so choose a strap-on stand that is less conspicuous to deer.

Tree-Stand Safety

Make safety your first consideration whenever hunting from an elevated stand. Each year, many hunters are injured or killed in falls. To avoid becoming a statistic, follow these rules:

• Always wear a harness or safety belt (right). Allow just enough slack so you can sit down comfortably.

• Practice at home before using a stand during the hunt. Attach your stand to a tree or utility pole, 2 or 3 feet above the ground. Put all your weight on the edges of the stand, leaning out as though taking a shot. If the stand twists when you lean (a fairly common problem), now is the time to find out.

• Take your time when climbing or descending, and climb no higher than the elevation at which you are comfortable.

• Check all bolts, welds, rivets, chains or straps on portable tree stands before using them.

• Be extra careful when snow, rain or cold creates slippery climbing.

• Trees with smooth bark spell trouble for a portable stand user. Use extra caution when climbing aspen, maple or other species with "slippery" bark.

• When using screw-in steps, be sure each step is screwed firmly into solid wood. The back of the step should snug up tightly against the tree trunk.

• Use a pull-up rope to raise and lower your unloaded gun or bow.

• Always let someone know exactly where you are hunting and when you plan to return.

Strap-On Stands

Advantages:

• Inexpensive, so you can afford to erect several and move between them as conditions change.

• Easy to carry and erect.

• Can be used in any tree sturdy enough to hold your weight, regardless of how the trunk and branches are arranged.

• Fairly inconspicuous; can be left in the tree (where legal) and secured with a chain and padlock.

Disadvantages:

• Many steps or a long section of ladder are needed to reach high stand positions.

• No body support rails – just a foot stand and small seat. Lack of supports may cause hunters to feel insecure, affecting their concentration and confidence.

Ladder Stands

Advantages:

• Easy to erect and climb.

• Safe and sturdy.

Disadvantages:

• Expensive.

• Too heavy and bulky to be conveniently portable.

• Looks out of place and obvious at close range; may spook deer.

• May invite use by other hunters.

• Uncomfortable; many have no seats, forcing the hunter to stand or sit on a small platform.

Self-Climbing Stands

Advantages:

• No steps or ladders needed.

• Can be quickly climbed to considerable heights.

• Sturdy, safe and comfortable; may have body support bars, rifle shooting supports, and adjustable seat height.

• Hunter can wear safety belt while climbing and sitting.

• Can be "walked" around tree while in use to take advantage of changing winds.

Disadvantages:

• Bulky, fairly heavy and awkward to carry.

• Noisy to erect.

• Requires some physical strength to erect.

• Cannot be used in trees with low branches.

Tripod Stands

Advantages:

• Good in short brush where there are no tall trees.

• Can be erected nearly anywhere.

• Easy to climb.

• Swivel seat provides comfortable seating.

• Support bars provide steady gun rests for long shots.

Disadvantages:

• Expensive.

• Heavy and bulky.

• Erecting the stand is time-consuming and noisy.

• Obvious to other hunters and deer.

Permanent Stands

Advantages:

• Can be large and sturdy enough to accommodate two hunters; ideal for teaching young hunters.

• Comfortable; may include rests for aiming guns or holding bows, and roofs and sidewalls for hunting in bad weather.

• Quiet in use; no chains or pipes to rattle.

• Safe, if built and maintained properly.

Disadvantages:

• Highly visible; draws attention to hunting location and often invites use by other hunters; many deer never become comfortable with its presence.

• Can be noisy if branches squeak against boards or nails.

• Needs maintenance; dangerous as they age or rot.

• Illegal in many areas.

Tree-Limb Stands

Advantages:

• Convenient; any large trees with sturdy horizontal limbs can be used.

• Quiet; no chains or pipes to rattle.

• Doesn't spook deer, as do some elevated portable stands.

• Other hunters can't pinpoint where you're hunting.

Disadvantages:

• Requires a suitable tree with large, sturdy limbs.

• Uncomfortable when used for long periods.

• Difficult and dangerous to shoot from, if footing is uneven or bark is wet.

A DEADFALL with lots of branches creates a quick ground blind. Make sure you're able to move your weapon freely for a clear shot.

Ground Stands

Although hunters are usually less detectable in elevated stands and can peer more easily into woods and brush, ground stands also have advantages. Using an elevated stand often requires that you remove many branches – a noisy operation that may frighten deer. And in areas where tree-stand hunting is rampant, deer may be more alert to danger from above than from below. In any habitat where visibility is greater from the ground, such as a pine plantation, a ground stand is more practical than one that is elevated.

Ground stands may be your only option if you can't climb for physical reasons, or if you're a rifle hunter in a state that prohibits the use of elevated stands.

A ground stand can be as simple as a wide tree trunk beside a trail, or as elaborate as a box blind elegantly equipped with heaters, chairs and sliding glass windows. Such fancy blinds can be effective if you're a rifle hunter able to make long shots, but most bow and gun hunters do better by trying to blend into natural cover without noticeably disturbing the area.

Ground Stand Types

PIT BLINDS, simple holes dug in the ground, are effective in open country with little ground cover.

ARTIFICIAL BLINDS set up easily and are relatively inexpensive. Use them near deer crossings, where natural cover is too sparse to break up your outline.

HAY BALES can be positioned to conceal hunters watching the edges of feed fields.

CORNSTALKS left standing in harvested fields provide excellent spots to ambush deer feeding in late afternoon.

CONIFERS with thick, low branches can be trimmed to make enough room for a sitting or kneeling hunter.

ABANDONED BUILDINGS and farm machinery make ideal ground stands because deer are already accustomed to them.

27

How to Stand-Hunt

Successful stand-hunting requires three skills: knowing where to position your stand; learning how to enter and exit it without alerting deer; and understanding how long to hunt the site before abandoning it in favor of a new location.

When choosing a stand location, consider wind direction first and foremost. To ensure that your scent does not alert your quarry, set up downwind or at worst crosswind, from the direction you expect deer to approach. Elevated stands can sometimes carry your odor over deer, but don't rely on this. If in doubt about wind direction, squirt scent-free powder (p. 18) or toss a pinch of milkweed down into the air to test the breeze.

If you hunt where prevailing winds are from the northwest, establish your stand to the southeast of where you expect deer to pass. We recommend you choose an alternate stand for days when the wind blows from the opposite direction. If conditions won't allow you to set up downwind, save the location for another day and hunt a different area instead.

If possible, place your stand so that the low sun will shine from behind you, effectively blinding your quarry. The best location for a morning stand, then,

is to the southeast of where you expect to see deer; in the evening, position your stand to the southwest – but only if the breeze allows.

Don't set up too close to where you expect deer to appear; whitetails can meander many yards off the predicted route – far enough to pass behind you if you're in too tight. A hunter who sets up too close may find himself twisting painfully in his tree stand, trying to get a shot at a buck walking just slightly off its anticipated course. And the closer you are to game, the greater the odds it will hear, smell or see you.

A gun hunter should stay as far back as the terrain, the cover and his killing accuracy permit. In open cover, this distance might be 50 to 100 yards for a shotgun or muzzleloader, or as much as 200 yards for a centerfire rifle. But in heavy cover, the best distance might be no more than 30 yards, regardless of the firearm.

Bowhunters are more constrained. Because they must get closer than gun hunters, camouflage and odor control are important concerns (p. 104). Drawing a bow without being noticed is always difficult, so an archer should follow the same advice given riflemen: set up as far away as your shooting abilities permit. You're more likely to get a good

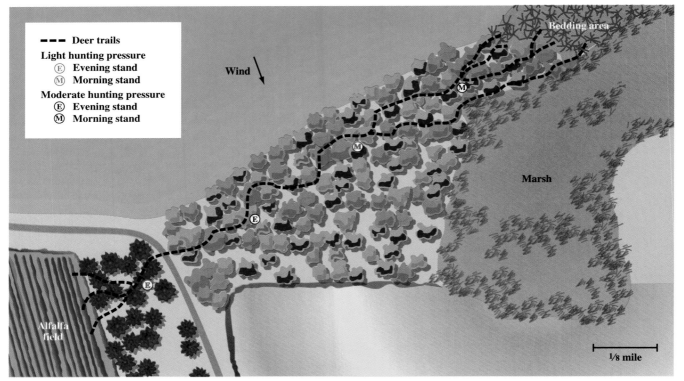

MOVE stand positions closer to bedding areas as hunting pressure increases. Bucks under pressure arrive at feeding sites later in the evening and leave them earlier in the morning. As shown above, both evening and morning stands must be closer to the bedding area in order to intercept bucks during legal shooting hours.

CHOOSE stands within shooting distance of deer trails marked with rub lines when hunting pressure is light (●). Under moderate pressure, bucks alter their movement patterns away from open areas, so choose stands in thicker cover adjacent to deer trails (●).

CURVES in trails are ideal locations for stands, because deer moving around bends tend to focus on the trail in front of them rather than looking side to side, as they do when traveling straight. In the trail mapped above, location A is a good spot for a stand when the wind is from the south, west or east; location B is a better choice when the wind is from the north. Cut narrow shooting lanes to provide clear broadside and quartering-away shots.

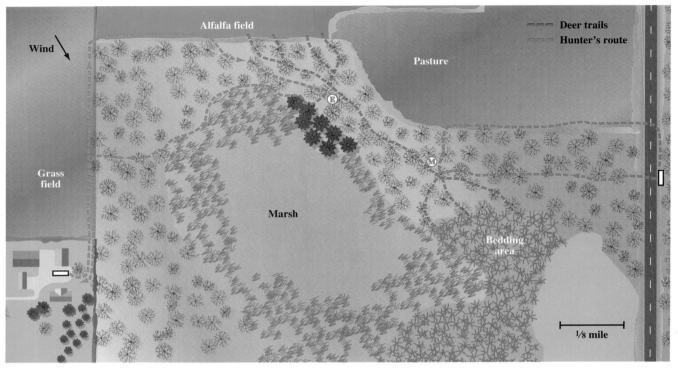

APPROACH an evening stand (Ⓔ) by walking field edges. Once in the hardwoods, don't walk on deer trails – instead, hike parallel to the trail on the downwind side. When exiting the stand, stay in the woods to avoid spooking deer feeding on the alfalfa field. Approach a morning stand (Ⓜ) through the hardwoods, but exit by walking along the pasture, steering well clear of the bedding area.

shot at a relaxed, unsuspecting deer at 25 yards than at 7 yards. So if you're skilled enough to keep all your shots inside a 6-inch circle at 25 yards, then go for it.

Once you've found the perfect stand site, you must enter and exit like a ghost – no odor, no noise, no red flags. Don't run to your stand fifteen minutes after sunrise and clamber up the tree like a lineman, equipment jangling. Sneak in while it's dark, taking whatever roundabout route necessary to avoid crossing game trails, feed fields, oak flats and other places where deer might see you or cross your scent. In late afternoon, you may pass through feeding sites en route to the stand, but avoid bedding areas at all costs.

You must exit without fanfare as well. For example, if you set a morning stand too close to a buck's bedroom, the animal might choose to lie down 50 yards away – too far away to be shot by bow, but too close to ignore 180 pounds of hunter sliding out of a tree.

Some hunters become so dependent on tree stands that they miss some great opportunities. If you come across hot buck sign, such as a cluster of fresh scrapes reeking of scent, don't run home for a portable tree stand. Instead, note the wind direction and select a good ground blind with enough brush to break up your outline. Hunt it immediately!

Stand-hunting is without question the most effective means of taking a trophy buck. Remember the following tips and you'll be well on your way to success:

• The first time you hunt a stand is usually the most productive, so don't waste this opportunity. Make sure conditions are prime. And never hunt the same stand more than two days in a row. Die-hard trophy hunters use a stand site no more than a few times in an entire season.

• If you are a gun hunter, elevate a tree stand as high as is comfortable. The higher you are, the less chance you'll be detected by passing deer. Bowhunters, however, should stay low enough to make double-lung shots.

• If the wind switches so you're upwind, don't wring your hands and hope – move to another location.

• Don't be predictable. Approaching and exiting your stand from the same direction each time allows deer to pattern *you*.

• Play your hunches. Move your stand when some insight tells you it's time. Hunting is as much intuition as it is science.

The Ultimate Portable Tree Stand?

If you're like most hunters, you have access to three or four tracts of land and have a couple of hot spots picked out at each property. Ideally, each of these spots should have at least two alternative stand sites from which you can choose, depending on wind direction. But who can afford a dozen portable stands, costing $60 to $150 each?

The solution? Many of North America's best whitetail hunters build their own stands – and you can too. Not only will you save money, but you can create stands with features specific to your needs.

The ultimate portable stand won't be the same for every hunter. So before you run to the local hardware store, analyze your hunting style. For example, if you can't stand on your feet for three or more hours at a time you'll want a stand with a seat. If your normal shooting stance is as wide as your shoulders, the stand's platform must be even wider. And if you hunt on land where your stand may "find legs and walk," you'll want a stand that can be locked to the tree with a chain and padlock.

The inexpensive and lightweight portable stand shown here has a small platform, making it easy to carry through brush, with a rope and no-tie rope cleat attachment system for totally silent setup. You can build as many as you want for under $20 each. The components can be purchased at hardware stores and marine supply outlets.

How to Erect the Stand

WRAP the rope around the tree and through the hole in the stand, with the stand angled downward.

THREAD the rope through the cleat, keeping the stand at the same downward angle.

LIFT up on the front edge of the stand to sink the metal prongs into the tree. Bury the point of the support brace into the tree, and you're ready to hunt.

31

Driving

An old hunter with a reputation for organizing successful deer drives described his technique succinctly: "You can drive a whitetail buck anywhere it wants to go."

That's the key to deer drives. Anticipate where the deer want to go and nudge them in that direction.

Hunters have been driving game over cliffs, into traps and toward ambushes for thousands of years. It's one of the oldest hunting tactics in the book, and it works because prey animals naturally flee from predators. Bedded whitetails normally remain hidden, but the sight, sound or odor of humans almost always scares deer into moving and exposing themselves. Hunters with knowledge of whitetail behavior and escape routes can drive the animals toward waiting companions posted strategically along the escape route.

Driving Basics

Practiced mostly by gun hunters, driving is a technique that works best near the end of the hunting season, when deer pressured by weeks of hunting spend most of the daylight hours bedded in thick cover. Because driving can disrupt normal deer activity patterns, reserve this method for the last day or two. Early in the season, deer are relaxed and trusting, living predictable patterns – this is the time to stand-hunt or still-hunt. When the start of the firearms season begins to spook deer, watch trails and cautiously still-hunt. During the rut, when bucks routinely prance through their territory in broad daylight, is another great time to stand-hunt or still-hunt. But in the weeks after the frenzied rut, bucks are usually bedded and can be nearly impossible to see. Now is the time to drive.

While drives can work throughout the day, they are most effective during midday, when the normal morning deer movement is over and the evening travel is yet to come. Deer are usually bedded in known locations at midday, and a party of hunters can fill these hours with two or three strategic drives.

Although forests are traditional locations for drives, you can successfully drive almost any habitat, including cattail sloughs, grain fields, tall grass fields, river bottoms, small wood lots and even prairie draws.

Planning a Drive

The first consideration when planning a drive is to choose a drive leader. The hunter with the most experience in the area is usually the best choice, because he knows where deer hole up and where they run when disturbed. The leader will lay out the driving plan, which the other hunters must follow to the letter (below).

Drive leader instructing other hunters

Small woods surrounded by fields

The second decision is choosing the hunters you want to participate. We strongly suggest you invite only hunters who can be trusted to cooperate fully and stick with their assignments. A single hunter who varies from the plan can ruin the hunt and threaten the safety of the whole party.

Big drive parties are seldom as productive as small groups of no more than six participants. Even two hunters can stage a successful drive. Novices imagine massive lines of hunters sweeping waves of game before them, but in reality, large gangs are difficult to coordinate, impossible to control and sometimes dangerous. The inevitable noise of a big drive getting into position alerts experienced bucks, causing them to sneak away. On rare occasions, however, such as when hunting a vast stretch of unfamiliar forest, large numbers of hunters moving in a line can roust out deer that would be nearly impossible to locate any other way.

When planning a drive, first study aerial photos or topographical maps of the area, or look at sketches made by someone familiar with the terrain. Like a war general, plan your moves on this map, selecting coverts small enough to be effectively driven. Dense, isolated pockets of brush and woods surrounded by large farm fields (left) will probably harbor bedded deer. And a brushy fenceline or drainage ditch leading from that core area to a distant swamp will be a natural escape route for whitetails.

Mark the map to indicate where you expect to see deer and where they're likely to flee. Draw each participant's starting location and assigned moves, noting starting points, starting times and assembly areas.

Divide your party into drivers and posters. Appoint only as many drivers as needed to push bucks toward the stationary posters. It's better to have too many posters covering all possible escape routes than to have too many drivers. Drivers should be in good physical condition; older hunters, or those with physical limitations, should be assigned as posters. Caution both the drivers and posters to shoot safely (opposite page).

Consider topography, cover types, escape routes and wind direction when planning the direction of the drive. Although some hunters insist that bucks always travel into the wind and that posters must locate upwind of all drives, these drives, in fact, are rarely successful. The reason is simple – as soon as the posters move into position upwind, bucks detect the hunters and move to avoid them. In reality, deer under pressure often keep the wind at their backs so they can use scent to detect danger from behind while using their eyes and ears to look ahead. As a result, we've found that drives which move deer downwind are usually the most successful.

To begin a drive, drop the posters off first. This gives them time to slip into position quietly and lets the woods quiet down after their intrusion. Allow at least 10 minutes before beginning the drive; 15 or 20 minutes is better, but don't drag things out too long or your posters may become restless or cold.

If you must position posters upwind, make sure they take measures to eliminate or cover their scent, just as a cautious bowhunter would do. Shower with scentless soap, use no perfumed colognes or lotions and wear clean clothes that have been stored in scent-free bags (p. 104).

Whenever possible, put posters in elevated positions, such as tree stands. A tree stand increases a poster's chances for spotting deer, and because his weapon is aimed downward, it also decreases the chance that a shot will go wild.

Drivers also should move into position quietly and quickly. Slammed car doors and loud voices encourage experienced deer to escape or hide in dense cover before the drive even gets underway.

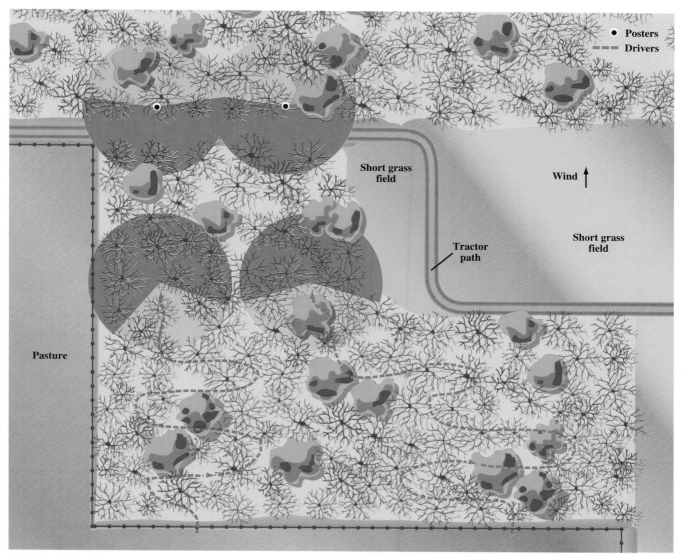

Short grass field

Wind ↑

Short grass field

Tractor path

Pasture

● Posters
- - - Drivers

NEVER SHOOT in the direction of other hunters, regardless of distance or thickness of cover. In the drive shown above, the safe shooting zones for drivers and posters are shown in blue; shots taken in all other directions (red) are dangerous. Drivers should not shoot toward the pasture or short grass field – areas beyond their vision. Posters can greatly increase their safe shooting zone by sitting in tree stands at least 15 feet high, waiting for deer to approach close enough for shots angled downward.

Once the driver farthest down the line is in position, he whistles the start command, which is then passed up the line. Drivers now begin walking their assigned routes, zigzagging to cover more territory and focusing on the heaviest cover, where crafty old bucks are likely to be hiding. Drivers should walk at a normal pace, stopping now and then to unnerve bedded deer. If the cover is too thick for drivers to see one another, have them shout briefly to identify their locations.

The act of shooting at deer sandwiched between drivers and posters is inherently dangerous: don't do it. Drivers should shoot only if deer have circled back around them. Posters must know the direction from

which drivers are approaching, must positively identify targets, and should not fire until deer are past them, where they can direct their shots away from the drivers. Each hunter should understand his safe shooting lane and adhere to it absolutely.

Driving is one of the few hunting techniques that gives you a chance to tag those mature, nocturnal bucks that rarely show themselves during legal shooting hours. Knowing where these deer spend midday and anticipating where they'll move when pushed may give you a shot at the biggest buck in your area. And the feeling of coordinating a group of hunters into a successful driving team is one of the most satisfying experiences we know.

Types of Deer Drives

TAGALONG DRIVES take advantage of a whitetail's habit of circling downwind to catch a hunter's scent. Hunter A slowly walks into the wind, followed 100 to 300 yards back (depending on cover density) by Hunter B, who cautiously still-hunts for bucks circling behind hunter A.

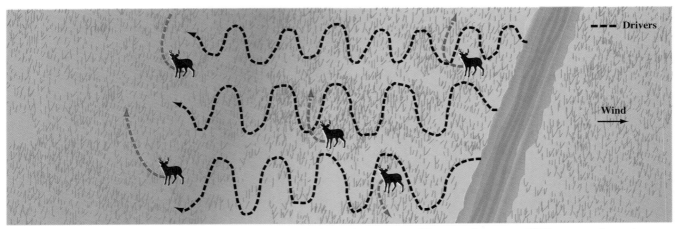

PHEASANT-HUNTER DRIVE works well in areas with short, dense cover, like new clear-cuts, CRP grass and marshes with low rushes. Drivers space 25 to 50 yards apart and walk a zigzag route, stopping frequently to unnerve bucks, which typically hold tight in such cover. No posters are needed, since deer usually don't jump until drivers are close.

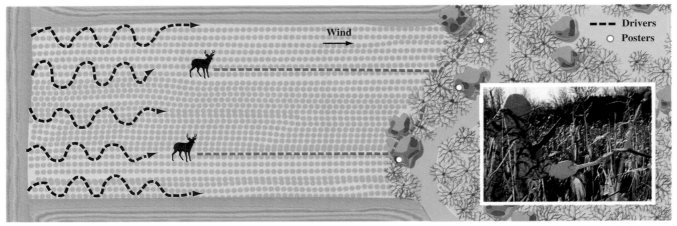

STANDING CORN DRIVE is often successful, since whitetails use cornfields as both dining room and bedroom. Drivers spaced no more than 30 yards apart zigzag across rows while slapping sticks against cornstalks to make plenty of noise (inset). Posters should be in tree stands if possible, for safety reasons. Drivers on each end of the line should walk 50 yards ahead to intercept deer fleeing out the sides of the field.

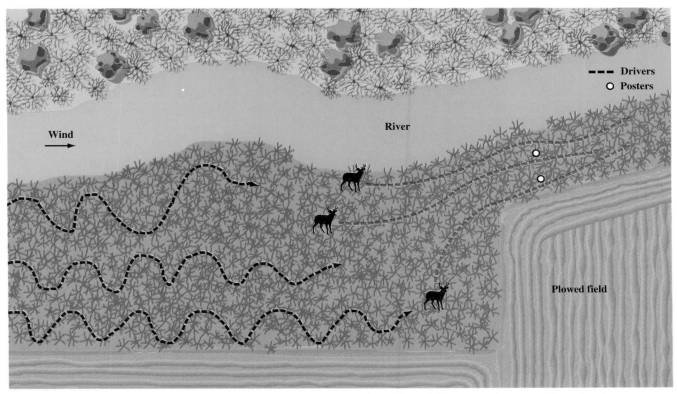

BARRIER DRIVES take advantage of natural or man-made obstacles to funnel deer toward posters. These barriers may include busy highways, lakes, rivers, open fields, clear-cuts and cliffs.

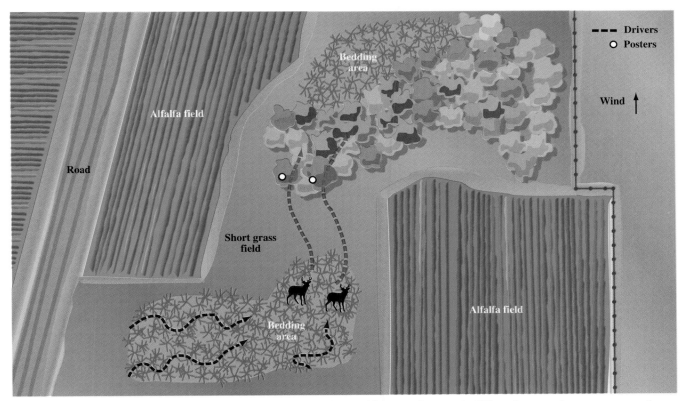

BOWHUNTER DRIVE uses posters set up in escape cover located in a nearby woods. When deer reach escape cover, they usually stop running and begin walking, offering a perfect target for waiting bowhunters.

Glassing & Stalking

According to guide Chris Yeoman of Rapid City, South Dakota, one thing in deer hunting is guaranteed: "If you can't see them, you can't shoot them."

In many types of habitat, including the rolling prairies, twisting river bottoms and broad grain fields where Yeoman hunts, the most effective method for finding wary old bucks is glassing with binoculars or a spotting scope. By magnifying his vision seven times or more, Yeoman "hunts" much more ground than he could on foot, often searching fields several miles away. And he accomplishes this without spreading human scent through a nervous old monarch's territory. "From a high vantage point, I can glass several feed fields or several miles of river bottom at once," the renowned guide explains. "When I spot a big buck, usually at the crack of dawn or at dusk, I note what he's doing....Then I try to guess where he's heading, plan my approach, and stalk or try to intercept him."

The tactic clearly works, if you judge by the number of trophy bucks Yeoman and his clients have taken over the years.

Glass and Stalk Basics

Obviously, glassing won't work in dense brush or woods, but we find it to be surprisingly effective in typical farm habitat, where open fields are interspersed with woods, ravines, lakes and sloughs – the kind of cover scattered widely across the Midwest and East. In mountain foothills or Texas hill country, careful searching with binoculars and spotting scopes can reveal moving or bedded bucks on dry, rugged slopes that are nearly impossible to hunt by other methods. In the rugged mountains of Arizona and New Mexico, most trophy Coues' whitetails are first spotted at long range, then stalked in their beds. And on the wide plains from Alberta through Oklahoma, glassing cuts down distances fast; hunters here sometimes locate bucks from 4 miles away.

To determine if glassing will work in your hunting area, study it during the off-season. Is there enough open space for clear viewing? Are there hilltops or ridges overlooking fields and open slopes? Any rimrock from which you could glass and shoot down into woods, brush or canyons? Are traditional deer trails, crossings and funnels visible and within shooting range? If the terrain will accommodate long-range viewing and the habitat makes it possible to stalk in for a shot, then you're in business.

Glassing can work in any season, but it's most likely to be successful during the rut, when bucks seeking mates often move across open country at any time of day. When glassing before the rut, look for bucks standing in shadows along the brushy edges of choice feed fields at dusk. In the days after the rut, look for hungry bucks feeding in undisturbed crop fields at dawn.

Equipment

To be an effective glass-and-stalk hunter, you need top-quality optics (p. 41), preferably both binoculars and a spotting scope.

Binocular magnification between 7× and 10× is most useful, with 8× being a good compromise. Binoculars more powerful than 10× are difficult to hold steady by hand. Some Coues' deer hunters use 15× or 20× binoculars during their all-day searches, but they usually mount them on tripods. The average hunter is better served by smaller binoculars that can be worn comfortably around the neck – something in the 7 × 35, 8 × 42, or 10 × 40 range.

Compact binoculars (7 × 24, 8 × 26, 10 × 28, for example) are popular because of their light weight, but because the lenses are smaller, compacts are inherently less bright. Expensive compact binoculars, constructed from top-quality glass with superb resolving power, can be fine for daytime glassing, but in low-light conditions, we've found full-size binoculars to be a better choice.

Spotting scopes have a longer optical reach than binoculars, with magnifications ranging from 15× to 60×. With a spotting scope on a tripod, you can identify bucks at distances up to 4 miles, and at closer range, you can count antler tines to accurately assess a buck's trophy potential.

Some scopes have zoom eyepieces that let you vary the magnification. Use low settings for general searching, then turn power up for a closer look. Magnifications above 25× are effective only if the scope is of highest quality, and only on cool, clear days, when distortion is minimal.

Window-mounted support for use with a spotting scope or large binoculars

A spotting scope is virtually impossible to hold steady by hand, so mount your scope on a tripod that holds the scope at eye level as you sit comfortably on the ground. Avoid tall tripods, which are often unstable and can be jiggled by the merest breeze. In farm country, where you can search for deer while driving on country roads, use a scope mount designed to clamp onto vehicle windows (above).

Any legal weapon can work in conjunction with glassing, but because shots are often long, a hunter armed with a scoped, centerfire rifle has the advantage. A hunter armed with a bow, shotgun or muzzle-loader faces a tougher challenge: he must either crawl within range of an alert, bedded buck or precisely anticipate the best spot to intercept a traveling buck.

Because terrain and habitat are varied, a versatile rifle/scope combination is best. Flat-shooting, long-range calibers from 25-06 Rem. to 300 Win. Mag. carry enough energy to kill quickly at a distance (p. 43).

Equip your rifle with a sharp, bright, variable scope, something in the 2× to 8× or 3× to 9× range. You may need to accurately and confidently place the cross hairs on a buck's chest at 300 yards as it stands in shadowy brush. Or, you might have to aim down a small tunnel through branches at 100 yards in dim light.

Blinds and scent control usually aren't necessary during glass-and-stalk hunting because your target is generally far away. But quiet clothing, especially boots, can be important when stalking. Use camouflage clothing, where it is legal. Moccasins or padded boot covers are useful when completing the last stage of a sneak.

How to Glass and Stalk

Glass-and-stalk hunting is simple in theory. First, position yourself where you can watch the most likely game sites; then spot your buck and try to predict its movement; and finally, move into range and take your shot. What could be easier? In practice, you'll find that this strategy can become a little more complicated.

First, you must find the best vantage point. Elevation is the key. Hilltops, ridges and rimrock can provide excellent vantage points. You can even use a barn roof, silo or windmill tower, if you can find a farmer who'll let you risk the climb. The higher you can get above surrounding land and cover, the better you'll see into it.

SHOOTING SUPPORTS, such as bipods (above), monopods, cross sticks and walking staffs, can greatly extend your accuracy range.

Understanding Optics

To become an effective glass-and-stalk hunter, you need top-quality binoculars or a good spotting scope.

Binoculars are lightweight and easy to to use, making them a good choice when you'll be walking long distances or when you need to shoot quickly. Spotting scopes let you recognize objects at a greater distance, but are bulky and much heavier, and they take time to set up. A tripod, window clamp or some other means of support is essential for holding the scope steady.

When purchasing optics for hunting, consider the following:

• **Magnification** – The "×" rating of your optics signifies its magnification power. A pair of 7× binoculars, for instance, magnifies an object 7 times its actual size. Binoculars are usually rated from 6× to 10×; spotting scopes, 12× to 60×. Some spotting scopes have variable power, enabling you to zoom in for a close-up view.

• **Brightness** – This is an important consideration if you'll be hunting under dim-light conditions. Brightness depends mainly on the exit-pupil size of your optics, a number determined by dividing the diameter (in millimeters) of the objective lens by the power. In binoculars, the size of the objective lens is indicated by the second number of the "×" rating. A pair of 7 × 35 binoculars, for example, has a 35mm objective lens, so the exit-pupil size is 5. In spotting scopes, the size of the objective lens is not specified in the rating, but can be found by referring to the owner's manual.

In general, the higher the exit-pupil size, the greater the light-gathering capability and the brighter the image. If you demand optimum brightness for low-light viewing, buy binoculars and spotting scopes with 7mm exit pupils (the same size as a fully dilated pupil in the human eye). For adequate viewing up to one-half hour after sunset, a 5mm exit pupil will do. In broad

POPULAR OPTICS include: (A) 15× to 45× zoom spotting scope with tripod, (B) 10 × 42 and (C) 7 × 35 binoculars and (D) 10 x 25 compact binoculars

daylight, a 2.5mm exit pupil is sufficient. Compact binoculars, because of their small objective lenses, have a low exit-pupil size and are not a good choice for glassing in low light.

Other features that contribute to brightness are heavy, high-quality glass, and good coatings on all lens surfaces. Uncoated lenses reflect light, creating a hazy, indistinct image. Generally, the more expensive the optic, the brighter it will be.

• **Resolution** – The sharpness, or resolution, of the lenses is of major importance when choosing binoculars or scopes, and is determined mostly by the quality of the glass. A pair of 6× binoculars with excellent resolution is

more useful than a pair of 10× with poor resolution. Unfortunately, there's no direct method of measuring resolution, although price and manufacturer's reputation are good indicators.

• **Field of View** – Most optics manufacturers specify field of view in terms of feet at 1000 yards. In general, the higher the magnification, the smaller the field of view. A 60× spotting scope, for example, may have a field of view as narrow as 40 feet; a pair of 6× binoculars, 450 feet. While not a major consideration in most types of hunting, field of view becomes important when glassing close cover where a wide field of view makes it easier to spot game.

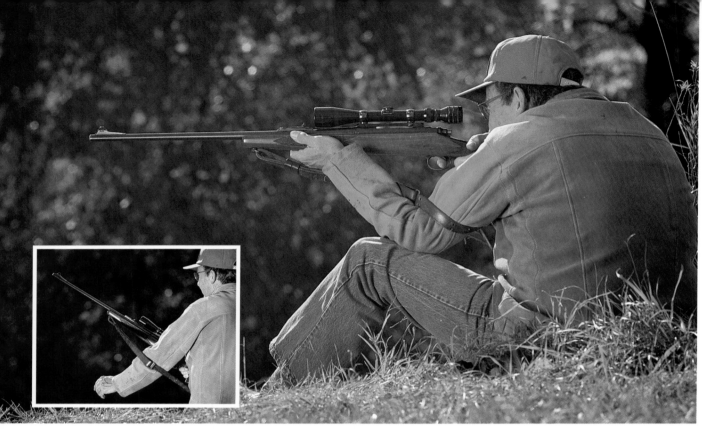

TRAIN yourself to shoot accurately using the *hasty sling* method. Start by wrapping your arm through the sling (inset) then grasping the forearm while resting your elbow on your leg. Objects like boulders, fence posts and tree trunks can be used when available, but the handiest, most reliable support is a practiced shooting form.

When hunting a new area for the first time, you'll want a long view. Arrive at first light and begin scanning likely looking meadows and fields – the places whitetails feed and frolic at dawn. Bright, sharp optics really help at this hour. Pan across each field quickly, starting with the closest. The oldest, largest bucks will be the first to move toward cover, so work quickly.

On your second and subsequent scans, the light will be better. Now you can spend more time checking corners and shadows, but continue to scan open areas as well. Glassing toward the rising sun – to the east and southeast – will silhouette deer against light backgrounds.

You can glass from several positions each day, if you're careful to minimize motion and noise, and use natural cover to hide your movement. At each glassing position, scour the terrain and cover – watch for unusual lines, the flick of an ear or tail, the glint of antlers or eyes. Deer activity usually falls off dramatically by midmorning and doesn't resume until late afternoon (unless bucks are rutting, or other hunters are in the field pressuring deer). At midday, focus your glassing efforts on bedding areas.

When you find a suitable target, begin your pursuit immediately. Stalk carefully, keeping wind direction in mind and using natural cover to disguise your approach. Before you move in, take note of major landscape features that will help orient your position in relation to the deer. Then use hills, banks, erosion gullies and thick vegetation to cover your movements.

If you repeatedly spot deer in the same general area but fail to reach them before they slip away, move your glassing site nearer their location. In heavy cover, you might narrow your search to a single field, or you can switch to stand-hunting or still-hunting. If you've seen a buck enter dense bedding cover, and it is rutting season, try to lure him out by rattling or calling.

As Chris Yeoman (right) and other successful whitetail guides will tell you, glass-and-stalk hunting offers huge rewards. Spying a peacefully unaware buck from a mile or more away, then stalking in silently for a killing shot, is one of the most exciting, adrenaline-pumping experiences you'll ever find.

Shooting

As a long-range hunter, you must shoot with great accuracy, a feat that requires an excellent eye, a steady hand, and a good rifle that has been carefully sighted.

Of all gun types, bolt actions are the most accurate. For maximum long-range performance, barrels should be 24 inches long to wring the ultimate velocity from each powder charge. Actions should be epoxy-bedded for tight and consistent fit. According to most bench-rest shooters, barrels shoot best if free-floated so they don't touch the stock, but some shooters like a pressure point at the tip of the fore-end stock.

Most rifles prefer one load of ammunition over all others. Hand-loaders know this and try several to find the best. If you shoot factory ammunition, sample several until you find the most accurate. The best bullets for long-range shooting are sharply pointed and long in relation to their diameter. Boat-tail designs outperform flat-base bullets at extreme range.

To range-test your gun, shoot from a solid bench with sandbags supporting the rifle to minimize human error. From the bench, the gun should consistently print three shots inside 1½ inches at 100 yards (inset above). From field-shooting positions, you should be able to keep three shots inside a 10-inch circle; the range at which you can no longer do this, whether 100 yards or 400 yards, should be your self-imposed long-range shooting limit.

Another skill worth developing is the ability to shoot quickly as well as accurately. A buck that momentarily walks across a small clearing can be yours if you can quickly place the cross hairs on his vitals. Shooters who depend on bipods or other shooting supports often miss these opportunities.

So-called flat-shooting calibers, like 270 Win., perform best if sighted to strike about 3 inches high at 100 yards. This puts them dead-on at about 230 to 250 yards, and only 4 to 6 inches low at 300 yards. Because a deer's vital chest cavity offers a target about 10 inches in diameter, aiming at its vertical center results in a killing shot at all distances out to 300 yards. At longer distances, a hold just on the deer's back line will drop the bullet into the heart/lung zone.

In contrast, a 100-yard sight-in would put the bullet 4 inches low at 200 yards and more than 1 foot low at 300 yards. You'll be tempted to "hold over" at distant targets, and if you guess wrong, you'll shoot high.

If these adjustments don't improve your rifle's groups, have a gunsmith "blueprint" the action by squaring the bolt face and action to the bore of the barrel. Older guns that shoot poorly might simply need a thorough cleaning with copper-remover solvent. Follow directions on the bottle.

Optimum Sightings for Long-range Efficiency

Cartridge	Bullet Size	Muzzle Velocity	Sight-In Yardage	Trajectory (yds.)			
				100	200	300	400
25-06 Rem.	120 gr.	2900 fps	240 yds.	+2.7	+1.9	-4.7	-18
270 Win.	140 gr.	2900 fps	243 yds.	+2.7	+1.9	-4.3	-17
280 Rem.	150 gr.	2800 fps	234 yds.	+2.7	+1.7	-5.4	-20
7mm Rem. Mag.	150 gr.	2900 fps	242 yds.	+2.7	+1.9	-4.4	-17
30-06	165 gr.	2800 fps	234 yds.	+2.7	+1.7	-5.4	-20
300 Win. Mag.	165 gr.	3000 fps	250 yds.	+2.6	+2.0	-3.6	-15

Snow-Tracking

Some hunters claim to be interested in deer tracks only if a big whitetail buck is still standing in them. That old joke may be good for a laugh, but it also demeans the art of tracking, an ancient hunting tactic that has hung more than one heavy rack over the barn door.

African bushmen are said to be incredible trackers, able to follow a mouse over a grassy savannah in the pouring rain. By contrast, some North American deer hunters are lucky if they can backtrack well enough to find their parked trucks. Fortunately for us, it often snows in the north during deer season, creating conditions that make it easier to locate deer – and our vehicles.

A fresh snow is like a road map guiding you to a buck. Follow those big tracks doggedly and you'll

How to Identify Fresh Deer Tracks

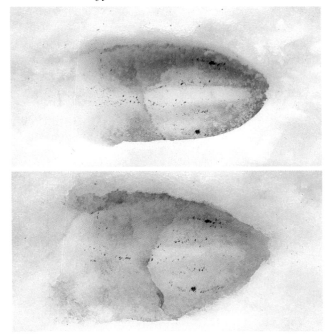

FRESH TRACKS (top) in snow have sharp edges; the snow on the bottom of the tracks is packed, but not frozen. Older tracks (bottom) tend to enlarge and crumble along the edges as they melt; the bottom of the tracks may be glazed with ice.

eventually catch up to their maker. But you must be in good physical shape and know how to read deer sign like a book. You also need to be persistent; after tracking a buck all afternoon, only to run out of daylight, you may be forced to pick up the trail at dawn the next day.

Snow-Tracking Basics

The best season for tracking is during the rut, and the best time to start is at dawn. Hunting during the rut means that your quarry will be on his feet much of the day looking for a doe, rather than lying in bed watching for trouble. And starting at dawn gives you all day to find a fresh track and follow it to the buck.

Snow-tracking is best after a fresh, 1- to 2-inch snowfall that has just ended. Under these conditions, old tracks will be covered, fresh tracks will show clearly and you can move at a good pace.

Falling snow can be good, too, if it isn't coming down so fast that it obliterates tracks before you catch up with their maker. Tracking in deep snow, however, can be an exhausting ordeal.

The best habitat for snow-tracking is open woods, where you have cover in which to hide but can still see far enough to spot and shoot your quarry at long range before it hears, smells or sees you. Farm country interspersed with woods and brush is also good, especially if it has hills you can use to hide your approach. Avoid flat terrain, which provides too many opportunities for an alert buck to spot you, and dense cover, where it's almost impossible to track a buck without him hearing you and hightailing it.

Snow-tracking works best in an area with low deer density, but good buck-to-doe ratios. In heavily populated areas, it's nearly impossible to track a single animal, because the ground usually is covered with a confusion of tracks.

Finally, you'll need elbow room. Try to get deep enough into public lands to have the place and its bucks to yourself. Nothing is so frustrating as following a hot buck track to a "No Trespassing" sign or to another hunter's fresh tracks.

TWO HUNTERS can cooperate in tracking a buck. While one hunter stays on the trail, the other flanks him, staying slightly ahead and watching alertly. A buck focused on watching its back trail may give the flanking hunter an open shot.

How to Snow-Track

Search for fresh tracks at the edges of feeding fields, along traditional trails or near known bedding areas. In country with many roads and few deer, you can scout by slowly driving through the countryside looking for tracks crossing the road.

Large tracks with drag marks usually indicate a buck (right). In snow deeper than 2 inches, however, any deer may leave drag marks. Urine spots dribbled between tracks are evidence of a buck on the move. This sign is usually found during the rut, when a buck searching for a doe may not stop to urinate.

When you identify big, fresh buck tracks, follow quickly but silently. Be alert, and try to imagine what the buck is doing and where he's going.

If his tracks run straight, he's walking steadily, perhaps to a scrape, a popular doe feed field or a bedding area. Hurry along the trail to catch up. If you think you know exactly where he's going, circle ahead to intercept him.

If the buck's tracks begin to meander, he may be browsing on limbs, sniffing doe tracks or poking his nose in the snow to find acorns. If there's no sign of feeding, a meandering trail suggests the buck is going to bed. In either case, now's the time to shift into low gear. If you suspect your buck is just ahead, check the breeze and circle to the downwind side of the trail. A buck that suspects he's being followed often loops around to check his back trail, and you may be able to ambush him if you've moved off his path.

Be persistent. If you work a big track all day and run out of light, return the next day to pick up the trail. If your efforts to snow-track a particular buck don't succeed, consider other strategies. By this time, you've learned enough about the buck's travel routes, feeding sites, scraping areas and bedding locations to still-hunt or ambush him from a stand.

When conditions are perfect, snow-tracking can be an unbeatable method for finding a whitetail buck. The right conditions may occur no more than one or two days each hunting season, however, so keep your skills honed and make the most of these chances. The most elusive trophy buck on the planet can't hide when the ground is blanketed with 2 inches of fresh white.

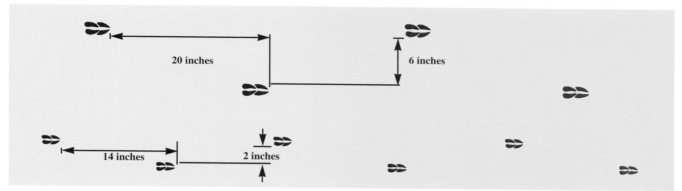

MATURE BUCK TRACKS (top) have an average stride distance of 20 inches, with about 6 inches between tracks. A doe (bottom) has an average stride of 14 inches, with only about 2 inches between tracks.

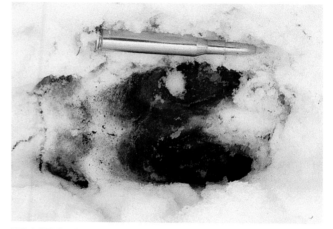

HOOVES of mature bucks (bottom) usually measure about 2¼ inches wide and have rounded tips. Doe and yearling buck hooves (top) are narrower and have more sharply pointed tips. In rocky terrain, however, any older deer can have worn hooves with rounded tips.

TRACKS of a big, heavy buck often have splayed toes and sink so far into the snow that the dewclaws are visible. Because females and fawns weigh much less than a mature buck, their tracks show splayed toes and dewclaws only if they were running.

DAYPACK contents for a long day of snow-tracking should include: (1) down vest, (2) first-aid kit, (3) rope, (4) toilet paper, (5) headlamp light, (6) map and compass, (7) whistle, (8) hand warmers, (9) candle, (10) waterproof matches, (11) folding saw, (12) knife, (13) candy bars, (14) sandwich, (15) water and (16) extra wool socks.

Rattling

"Rattling attracts whitetail bucks because white-tail bucks fight. It's just that simple." So says Larry Weishuhn, whitetail biologist, wildlife manager and hunting guide from Ulvalde, Texas. Thousands of successful rattlers from Idaho to Alabama will back him up.

Rattling – imitating the sounds of two bucks sparring with their antlers – began as a modern hunting technique in Texas thirty or forty years ago. On managed ranches where large numbers of bucks competed for smaller numbers of females, hunters soon discovered that mimicking a good whitetail fight could draw in those aggressive bucks as though they were on strings.

Why do bucks respond to the clash of antlers? Larry Weishuhn believes that aggression and frustration probably play a role. As the breeding season nears, mature bucks become intolerant of one another and begin spoiling for a fight. Although whitetails are not strictly territorial, bucks do spar to establish dominance within their range. When a big buck hears other bucks fighting, he'll often come running to show them who's really boss.

For a buck that doesn't yet have a doe, the motive for responding to the rattling call may be theft. When he hears the sound of two bucks fighting, the bachelor slips in to steal the doe while the other bucks are preoccupied.

Finally, bucks may simply be curious. Young bucks, in particular, just have to see what all the ruckus is about. Experienced bucks generally respond for more aggressive reasons.

FIGHTS between two mature bucks usually last less than a minute, with the winner claiming the hot doe as his prize.

Rattling Basics

Rattling works best in territory where there are many mature bucks competing for females. Competition is the key. Rattling is less successful in areas where overhunting has taken a heavy toll on bucks. In these circumstances, surviving bucks have so many females to pick from that they have no need to fight one another or respond to your rattling.

The absolute best time to "rattle in" a big buck is in the 10 to 14 days just before the first doe comes into estrus, known as the scraping period of the rut. Bucks are at their physical peak at this time, pumped up, ready to breed, and eager for that first doe to extend an invitation. In the meantime, males have nothing to do but take out their frustration on each other. Bucks responding to rattling during the scraping period usually arrive in a hurry and are spoiling for trouble – strutting stiff-legged, with hackles raised and ears laid back (right).

Once females come into estrus, rattling is no longer a sure-fire technique, but it's still worth using. Don't expect to rattle in a buck who's enjoying the company of a friendly female, but a male who is between mates and actively searching for one will be ready to fight at any time.

As the rut winds down, bucks suddenly find themselves without willing partners and may again be drawn to the lure of clashing antlers. The final window of rattling opportunity comes a month after the main rut. At this time, any unbred females once

again come into estrus, and some female fawns reach their first estrus.

Weather can make or break a rattling session. On a calm day, the sound of your rattling carries farther and will be heard by more bucks. On cloudy or foggy days with dim light, bucks are active later in the morning and earlier in the evening and are more

Mature buck responding aggressively to a rattling session

RATTLING ACCESSORIES include: (1) gloves, (2) face mask, (3) camouflage face paint, (4) synthetic antlers, (5) safety ribbon, (6) genuine antlers, (7) grunt call, (8) Fighting Buck System® and (9) rattling bag. Synthetic antlers have proven to work as well as the real thing; carry either when a major part of your hunting plan includes rattling. Stuffing antlers in a day-pack keeps them quiet and out of the way while walking. If you're planning to rattle only infrequently or as an emergency measure, the more portable rattling bag or Fighting Buck System is adequate.

likely to respond to rattling. Another excellent time to rattle is on the first clear, calm morning after a severe storm that has forced deer to hole up. Rattling is less effective on windy or rainy days, when the sound of your antlers is muffled.

Sunrise and sunset are good times to rattle, because deer are most active during these periods. But during the rut and in the days just preceding, eager males seeking mates are on their feet and moving most of the day. Many trophy bucks have been "rattled in" at midday.

If possible, set up near heavy cover or known bedding areas, where secretive big bucks spend most of their time. Choose a spot with good visibility in all directions – at least 20 yards for bow-hunters, and 50 to 75 yards for gun hunters. You should be able to see even farther than this in the downwind direction, because big bucks often circle to the downwind side when scent-checking the source of a noise. Other good places to rattle are near scrapes, along rub lines and along heavily traveled doe trails.

Any hunting technique that imitates the quarry has the potential to attract other hunters. In heavily hunt-ed areas, protect yourself by painting rattling antlers blaze orange or hot pink. Some hunters place a blaze-orange garment or wide ribbon around a tree trunk or overhead branch to alert other hunters attracted to their rattling. Even if you think you are the only hunter in the woods, *always* wear a blaze-orange hat and vest, even if not required by law. No buck is worth dying for.

How to Rattle

Once you've chosen a rattling site with a good view, make sure you have clear shooting in a complete circle. You don't want a limb interfering with a quick shot, so break off branches, if necessary, and don't worry about the noise you make; you're going to be imitating two battling, 200-pound animals in a few moments, so noise is expected. Pay particular atten-tion to the downwind side, where experienced bucks are likely to appear. Place cover scents downwind of your position and attractor scents to either side. In this way, a buck circling downwind of your position will be drawn in by the attractor scent before it catches your odor (p. 101).

If you can get into a tree stand, so much the better. You'll have a good view into the cover and your odor may be too high for your quarry to detect. Rattling from an elevated position may sound unnatural to some wary bucks, but it has successfully fooled hun-dreds of others.

If you combine rattling with stand-hunting from one location for several hours, limit your rattling to no more than one sequence each hour. If bucks are bed-ded within hearing and don't respond, frequent rat-tling makes them suspicious. But a single rattling sequence each hour won't spook bedded bucks and will attract bucks that recently moved into the area.

When deer aren't moving, the best approach is to combine rattling with still-hunting. Whenever you approach heavy cover, set up against a tree trunk or a bush to rattle. Wait about 15 minutes after a rattling

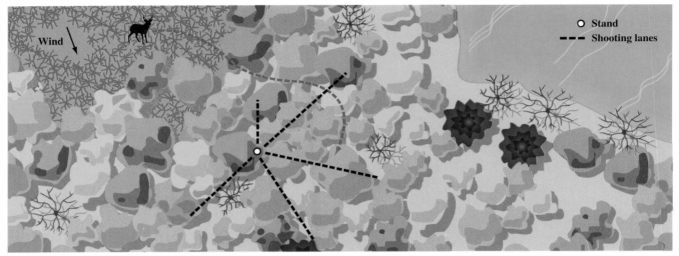

Legend: ○ Stand, --- Shooting lanes; Wind

CHOOSE a rattling location with good shooting lanes in all directions and downwind of thick cover used by bucks. Shoot as the buck circles downwind in an attempt to scent-check the area.

sequence, then move ahead 100 to 400 yards, depending on cover and weather conditions, and rattle again. Chances are you'll eventually tickle the tines within hearing range of a buck. Another way to convince a buck you're the real thing is to combine rattling with calling (p. 55) and decoying (p. 60).

Two partners can increase their chances for taking cautious bucks if one hunter sets up 50 to 100 yards downwind of the rattler. This downwind satellite

shooter can sometimes tag a sneaking buck as it circles back to work the wind.

There is no right and wrong way to mimic the sound of fighting bucks. One method for learning the sounds and rhythm of a buck fight is to rent a video that features a real knock-down-drag-out battle. Close your eyes and visualize what the bucks are doing as you listen to the tape. Some bucks fight like demons for a quarter hour or more, grunting and snorting and

Rattling Tips

BLOW on a grunt call before rattling to simulate the sound a buck makes when he is accompanying a doe.

MOVE the antlers slowly from one side to the other as you rattle, duplicating the sound of bucks moving during a fight.

RAKE saplings and strike the ground to mimic the sounds of breaking brush and hoof-stomping.

QUIT RATTLING when a buck is at close range. If you continue, he'll soon discover the source of the sound and flee.

crashing antlers like garbage collectors at five A.M. Others merely brush their antlers together a few times. The following scenario will start you in the right direction; modify it as you gain experience:

Once in position, familiarize yourself with the surroundings so you don't mistake a stump or shadow for an approaching buck. Place your gun or bow within easy reach. Grunt softly three times, then wait a few minutes. If a buck is close, sudden and aggressive rattling could spook him, but grunting rarely does. If nothing shows, rattle the tines lightly for 30 to 60 seconds, as if two mildly feisty bucks were toying with one another, sizing each other up. Wait a few more minutes. If nothing shows, begin a more aggressive sequence.

Expert hunters are divided on the best way to initiate the sounds of an aggressive buck battle. Some claim that whitetails don't butt heads as do sheep; these hunters recommend bringing the tines together gently, then twisting them aggressively. Other hunters who have seen and heard dramatic meetings between antlered titans suggest crashing the tines into one another, then twisting and rubbing.

Grasp the antlers firmly when rattling to produce an authentic sound. Wear tight-fitting leather gloves or gloves with rubber grips to keep your hands from slipping. Don't constantly clash the antlers; instead, try to work in quiet moments lasting about two seconds, followed immediately by more sound. This simulates the way fighting bucks surge and pause. Stomp your feet from time to time, rake brush and drag the antlers through the dirt and leaves, imitating the sounds of two rut-crazed bucks in an all-out fight. Begin rattling with the antlers on one side of your body, then slowly move them to the other side

to mimic the sounds of bucks moving during the battle. After a minute or so, stop rattling, set the antlers down, raise your gun or bow and scan the surroundings. Wait 5 to 10 minutes, then rattle one last time for a period of 1 to 2 minutes to complete the sequence.

True trophy bucks are notorious for responding slowly and cautiously, so if you're targeting such an animal, give him plenty of time to come in. If you're still-hunting, for instance, wait about 45 to 60 minutes at each rattling site (instead of the usual 15 minutes) before moving to a new location.

Don't rattle constantly or indiscriminantly, especially if you're after a big buck. Save the tactic for ideal conditions. As many trophy-buck hunters report, a young buck might respond to rattling several times, but an experienced deer quickly catches on to the ruse. If you fool a wise old monarch once or twice without taking him, chances are he'll ignore rattling for the rest of the season, possibly forever. A buck doesn't get old and big by being stupid.

Rattling isn't magic. It doesn't always work, but when it does, the excitement is unsurpassed. As Larry Weishuhn (right) notes, as long as bucks keep fighting for females, they'll respond to the lure of rattling.

Calling

Not long ago, hunters believed that the only vocal noises whitetails made were the alarm snorts blown when they ran from danger with tails flagging. Since then, a veritable whitetail language has been discovered, and hunters who learn to understand and speak it have yet another hunting tactic up their sleeves. Calling by itself isn't a sure-fire charm that will bring deer running right to your feet. But used in conjunction with still-hunting, stand-hunting and other techniques, we've found that a well-timed and well-executed call can be the difference between tagging your buck and going home empty-handed.

According to Will Primos (right) of Primos Game Calls, Native Americans were calling to attract whitetails hundreds of years ago, but the skill was largely lost until the latest whitetail hunting craze took off in the 1980s. Twenty years ago there were few  commercial whitetail calls on the market; today there are dozens, designed to mimic everything from the soft bleat of a fawn to the aggressive wheezing snort of a big, dominant buck. And these commercial calls do the job – provided you learn the whitetail language and know where and when to use it.

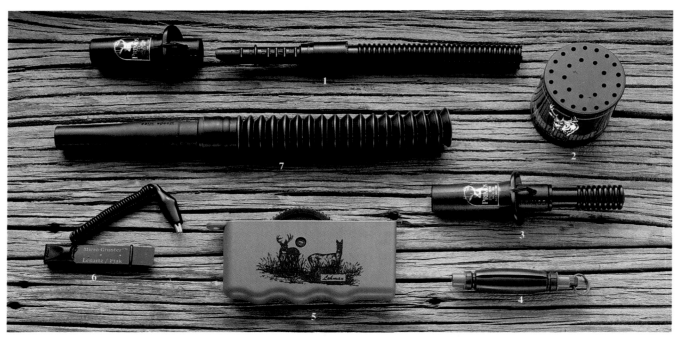

COMMERCIAL CALLS include (from top left): (1) adjustable grunt tube call, which can be varied to different pitches; (2) bleat call in a can, operated by tipping the can; (3) bleat call, a mouth-blown call that can be used without hands; (4) snort call, operated by forcibly blowing; (5) hand-operated grunt call, operated by rotating the wheel extending from the side; (6) micro-grunt call, which allows hands-free operation and is often used by bowhunters; (7) hyperventilator grunt call, which makes noise when the user inhales and exhales.

The Language of Whitetails

Whitetails vocalize about a dozen sounds, and although not every one is worth imitating, the hunter who understands the entire language gains a better understanding of whitetail behavior. From the hunter's perspective, it's helpful to divide these vocalizations into three categories: doe-fawn calls, alarm calls, and breeding calls.

DOE-FAWN CALLS. The sounds fawns and their mothers use to communicate with one another are usually heard during spring and summer. The *mew* and *nursing whine*, made by fawns, and the *maternal grunt*, made by females, are low in volume and of little use to hunters.

The fawn also makes a louder *bleat*, used to signal the mother when the youngster has become separated or wishes to nurse. A hunter mimicking this bleat can occasionally call in a doe or a buck looking for the source of the noise.

ALARM CALLS. Alarm calls include a variety of snorts and bawls. The *snort*, made when a deer forces short blasts of air through its nostrils, has several forms. Some snorts are high-pitched whistling sounds made by frightened deer fleeing an intruder. Others are lower in pitch and longer in duration; deer make this snort when they are alarmed but have not yet

figured out the source of the danger. Whitetails seem to use this lower-pitched snort, often accompanied by foot stomping, to startle a predator into revealing itself. The call also alerts other deer within earshot that they should be ready to run. A hunter can imitate an alarm snort as a last-ditch effort to stop a running deer, hoping it will pause and look around for the source of the sound.

A *bawl* is an intense alarm call made by traumatized deer, a sound similar to that of an infant baby crying. Usually made by younger deer, bawls will send most deer fleeing – except for nursing females, who may come running with blood in their eyes, ready to battle whatever is hurting the fawn. Imitating this sound is a desperation ploy you can sometimes use to lure in a doe, who may be accompanied by a buck.

BREEDING CALLS. These calls include at least four distinct grunting and snorting sounds heard during the rut. Breeding calls are the primary language of bucks, and most commercial calls are designed to imitate these noises. A hunter who learns how to accurately mimic these sounds has a decided advantage.

The *low grunt,* made by dominant deer of either sex, is a single, short call, low in pitch and volume, and audible only at short distances. Mimicking this call can sometimes draw in a buck that is just out of shooting range.

Bucks often make a grunt-snort wheeze just before fighting

The *tending grunt* is perhaps the most important call for hunters. It consists of an excited series of three to thirty drawn-out "urrrp urrrp urrrp" noises spaced 2 to 3 seconds apart, resembling the grunting of a barnyard pig. The tending grunt is made by a buck who is either trailing a mate or is already in the company of a doe. It may be the buck's way of warning other bucks to stay away, or it may simply express excitement; either way, it tells other bucks that there is action worth investigating. As research has shown, tending grunts are usually made by dominant bucks. Mimicking this call can quickly bring in the local big buck intent on fighting the challenger. Smaller bucks may come too, but more slowly and cautiously, hoping to get lucky without getting a bloody nose.

The *grunt-snort* is an intense "huhh, huhh, huhh, huhh" sound made when whitetails force air through their open nostrils in a series of three to six brief blasts, 1 to 2 seconds apart. The sound is much like the alarm snort. Grunt-snorts are given occasionally by females, but are most often made by bucks challenging rivals. Usually preceded by the low grunt, a grunt-snort indicates that the level of conflict between two deer has escalated. With hair standing erect and ears laid back, a dominant buck snorts with every step as he approaches his adversary.

The last breeding call in the whitetail's repertoire is the *grunt-snort wheeze*, an intense call heard when a buck is preparing for a major dominance fight. The call begins with a short, rapid series of grunt-snorts followed immediately by a drawn-out wheeze sounded as the buck forces air through his pinched nostrils: "huh-huh-huh-heeee." During these conflicts, a doe is almost always present, and a violent fight for breeding rights is likely.

Imitating a grunt-snort or grunt-snort wheeze won't call in many small bucks, but it just might lure in the most dominant buck in the area.

Calling Basics

Calling can be used successfully in any whitetail habitat. Like many tactics that imitate deer behavior, it is most productive just before and during the rut, that hectic time when bucks have plenty to say and are eager to listen to other deer. If you can make a buck believe you're a competing male, or a fawn with a mother nearby, you're in business.

The technique must be used carefully, however. If you say the wrong "words" or give the wrong inflection, you'll frighten deer away rather than attract them. Calling must be done at the right volume, in the right place and at the right time – otherwise, you might as well be whistling Dixie. Practice calling, preferably with another experienced hunter who can

Deer-Calling Volume

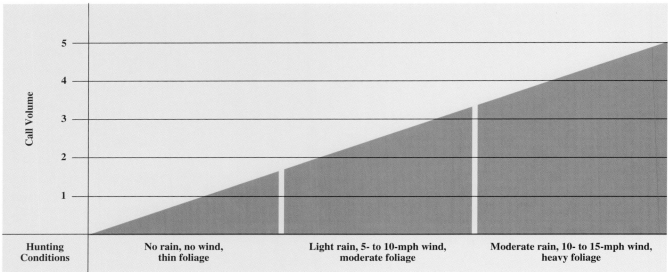

VOLUME recommendations for calling deer from 75 to 100 yards are shown above, on a scale from 1 to 5, with 5 being loudest. Call volume varies based on wind, rain and density of foliage. Under ideal conditions with no wind, rain or foliage to muffle the sound, a call of volume 1 is barely audible to a human at 20 yards; volume 5 is audible at 100 yards.

judge the accuracy of your mimicry. A good way to learn the language of whitetails is to rent a video that features deer making the various calls.

Calling is best used in conjunction with still-hunting or stand-hunting. As a rule, never call to a deer that is looking in your direction or coming your way, because whitetails have an uncanny ability to pinpoint sounds. Save your call for times when deer are in the vicinity but just out of range; your goal is to bring them close enough for a shot, not so close they're staring you in the eyes (right). Make your calls at random intervals, and don't call too often from the same location, since this sounds unnatural to deer. Humans tend to call too loudly for the sensitive ears of whitetails; tone it down, or your calls will frighten away most deer (above).

With eight or ten sounds at your discretion, which call do you pick? It depends on the circumstances. In most instances, you'll be trying to imitate breeding calls – the sounds most likely to interest rutting bucks. Commercial calls are available that mimic most whitetail calls, though some hunters vocalize the sounds themselves.

When you know there is a nearby buck just out of shooting range, blow a low grunt and wait for a response. Your buck will interpret the call as the voice of another male asserting his dominance, and will probably want to argue the point up close.

When a rutting buck is well out of shooting range, use a tending grunt call. To imitate the sounds made by a buck tending a doe, make a half-dozen grunts,

pause for a minute or two, then make a longer series of grunts, followed by a 15-minute break. There is no right or wrong cadence – the call might be quite fast or rather slow, continuous or interrupted – but the volume should be a couple of notches louder than the low grunt.

Buck looking at hunter in tree stand

TENDING GRUNTS are made by a buck following a doe in estrus. Hunters imitating this sound can fool bachelor bucks into believing a doe is nearby.

Grunt-snort and grunt-snort wheeze calls are especially effective when used with rattling to mimic the sounds of bucks battling over a doe. Begin by blowing a low grunt. Wait a few minutes, then switch to a snort call to make a series of "huhh, huhh, huhh" grunt-snorts before starting your rattling session. Or start with a tending grunt followed a few minutes later by a "huhh-huhh-huhh-heeee" grunt-snort wheeze made on a snort call, then begin the rattling. The goal is to paint an audio portrait of a buck who is being challenged into battle by another buck over the right to breed a doe. A real buck eavesdropping on this drama will be tempted to come in and steal the doe while the suitors are fighting over her.

Although breeding calls are normally the first choice of hunters, under special circumstances you might want to try doe-fawn calls or alarm calls.

If you spot a doe just out of range, for example, imitating a fawn bleat may rouse her maternal instincts and draw her toward you. If you're lucky, she may be followed closely by a buck. To imitate the fawn bleat, make three or four calls, spaced 3 to 4 seconds apart. Mimicking the bawl made by an alarmed deer can have the same effect on a nearby doe. To imitate this sound, cup your hand over your mouth, pinch your nostrils closed, and make a high moaning sound, descending in pitch and lasting 1 to 2 seconds. Wait for a few seconds, give another bawl; wait for 5 seconds, then give one last bawl. At times, a series of long, drawn-out bawls lasting 8 to 10 seconds can lure in a doe from a great distance.

As a last-ditch effort to stop a deer running away, you can mimic the snort of an alarmed deer. Give a very loud, single blast of air from your mouth, then remain absolutely silent and stand ready for one quick shot as the deer pauses to look for the origin of the call.

Calling isn't the final answer to deer hunting's mysteries, but it does add another dimension of realism in your bid to fool the whitetail. When used properly and combined with other deer-hunting strategies, calling can bring deer into easy gun or bow range.

Decoying

Thirty years ago there was a great joke in deer camp: "Did you hear about the city slicker who tried deer hunting? Gave it up after one day. Said the decoys were too heavy." For modern hunters, the joke no longer applies. Whitetail decoys are now a legitimate tool for fooling trophy bucks.

As bowhunting grew in popularity perhaps it was inevitable that someone would eventually try using a decoy to lure a buck within arrow range. And why not? In fall, a buck's focus is on romance. He's looking for either female companionship or a rival buck to battle. And when he sees a potential mate or a challenger – even an artificial one – he'll come running.

Decoys are the ultimate lure. Rattling and calling techniques are fine for drawing the attention of bucks, but an experienced, suspicious buck often stays out of range if he can't see what makes these sounds. Rattling and calling to arouse a buck's curiosity, then showing him a decoy, is a triple threat that's hard to beat.

Of course, as with any of man's attempts to mimic nature, deer decoys aren't perfect. They are bulky to transport, they don't move, and they don't smell like deer. But, while most of these drawbacks can be remedied, what can't be remedied is the fact that decoys draw attention from other hunters. For this reason, never use

DECOYS come in three basic types, most of which have removable antlers and can be converted from a buck to a doe. Three-dimensional, lightweight plastic foam decoys (left) mimic bedded deer; they can be rolled up and easily carried, but may blow in a heavy wind. Two-dimensional decoys (center) are hinged for easy carrying; they are convincing when viewed from the front, but do not look realistic when viewed from other directions (opposite page). Full-body hard plastic decoys (right) are realistic from any angle, but are bulky to carry long distances; some models feature adjustable ears and tails that can be set to mimic various whitetail moods, from alert to relaxed.

decoys during firearms seasons; for anyone who values his own life, decoying is strictly a bowhunter's game. Place a blaze-orange covering (below) over the decoy when transporting it in the field, and, at all times, *use extreme caution.*

Hunter carrying decoy in orange bag

Decoying Basics

Deer are naturally curious and gregarious animals that will respond to decoys at any time of year. But the best times to lure bucks are just before and during the breeding period, when bucks are driven to check out each doe they see and to argue with any other buck that pokes his nose into the area.

Early morning seems to be best for decoying. Deer returning home to bed after a calm night of feeding are contented and willing to socialize. And a disappointed buck, returning home after an unsuccessful night searching for a cooperative female, will eagerly respond to a doe decoy and aggressively approach a buck decoy.

Decoying can also be successful in the evening. Doe decoys placed in the corner of a feed field will often pull in a doe or two looking for company, and these live females may in turn draw in bucks.

As with calling and rattling, decoying is most productive near areas where bucks spend most of their time. Before and after the rut, this means placing your decoys at the edge of popular feeding fields, along major trails or near bedding areas. During the rut, set up decoys near scrapes, trails or rub lines. Don't move so close to bedding areas that you pollute them with scent, motion or sound, but do find a location that is close enough to tempt shy old bucks

Mel Dutton Decoys

A variation of the three-dimensional decoy is Mel Dutton's light-weight, plastic silhouette. Dutton (right), of Faith, South Dakota, pio-neered the portable

pronghorn decoy, and his whitetail decoy was a natural evolution. It can be used in a fixed position, but is at its best when manipulated by a hunter hiding behind it. Don't try this during any firearms season or where there are lots of bowhunters competing for deer. The Dutton decoy should be reserved for bowhunting on private land with controlled access.

This photo sequence shows a Dutton decoy in action:

1. The hunter has slipped cautiously downwind of where he expects a buck to be holding. He stakes the decoy in front of himself, places his bow within easy reach and begins rattling and/or calling.

2. When a buck slips into view but pauses in suspicion, the hunter shim-mies the decoy from side to side. This motion often convinces a buck the decoy is real.

3. The buck usually circles downwind to pick up scent. As it does, the hunter swivels the decoy on its stake, keeping behind it. When the buck presents a good target, the hunter rises to his knees, draws and shoots over the back of the decoy.

Crazy as it sounds, this method works, with the buck never quite realizing that the movement is caused by a predator. The method also works with two hunters, with one carrying a doe decoy, the other a buck. After setting up a few yards apart, one hunter draws an incoming buck's attention by moving his decoy, while the other hunter rises unseen to shoot. Safety is the first concern. Take no shots toward your partner – an arrow passing though the deer can be deflect-ed and exit on a different trajectory.

Trophy whitetail attacking a buck decoy

into slipping out and visiting your decoy during good shooting light.

Look for a spot where your decoy can be readily seen. A decoy erected on a hill or rise of ground will draw the eye of curious bucks. Open woods, field edges and small openings near thick cover also are good sites. Vegetation should be no more than 1 to 2 feet tall, so incoming bucks will clearly see the decoy. A bedded doe decoy is especially difficult to place for good visibility, so consider pairing your bedded decoy with a standing doe or buck decoy.

How to Use Decoys

Once you've found a good location, set up with the same care you'd use at any stand-hunting site. Move in with your gear as silently as possible, well before first light in the morning or before the magic evening travel hours.

Make sure to practice good scent control. Approach with the wind in your favor and don't walk where incoming bucks will cross your trail. To avoid contaminating the decoy, store it in a scent-free bag and handle it with rubber gloves. Spray it with scent eliminator before each hunt. To add realism, wire a pad saturated with natural whitetail urine to the decoy. During the rut, wire a fresh buck tarsal gland to the decoy's legs, or use a cotton ball saturated with an effective commercial estrus lure.

Movement can often make or break a decoy's effectiveness. If there's a breeze, hang a V-shaped white cloth over the decoy's tail and let it flicker. Some hunters rig a hinged tail or ear to the decoy

and activate it with fishing line stretching back to the shooting stand. You can also use fishing line to rustle brush next to the decoy, creating movement which may catch a distant buck's attention.

How you set up in relation to the decoy is critical. You generally want to be downwind, usually far enough so an approaching buck trying to circle downwind of the decoy will still be upwind of you. Before erecting the decoy, clear away stray branches from your shooting lanes. Use a tree stand, if possible, for its usual advantages. Refer to the accompanying illustrations for examples of typical setups.

When everything is in place, you can either wait for a buck to pass and see the decoy, or use rattling and calling techniques to draw his attention. When a buck sees the decoy and begins moving in, prepare yourself to shoot while his view is blocked, or while he is obviously mesmerized by the decoy. Don't rush the shot, but do take the first good opportunity. Although a buck usually circles a decoy, sometimes he'll charge a buck decoy; if you wait too long, the buck may knock over the decoy (above).

If you fail in your best efforts to lure a big buck, try using a two-decoy setup, with one decoy equipped with a very large set of antlers. Set the buck decoy beside the doe decoy; the combination should get the boss's attention.

Few hunting experiences are more entertaining than watching a big buck eagerly try to mate with a plastic doe, or angrily battle a plastic rival buck. By the time he discovers the ruse, your arrow is already on its way.

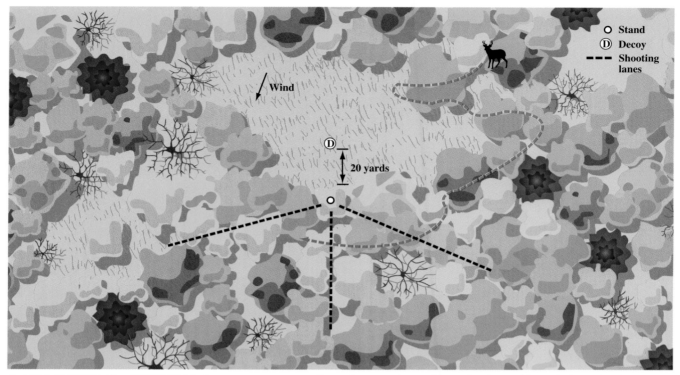

SMALL NATURAL OPENINGS in heavy cover are excellent places to decoy. Erect the decoy 20 yards from the down-wind edge of the opening; then take a stand downwind and just inside the cover. Make sure you have clear shooting lanes to the decoy, as well as to the right and left, where bucks may come sneaking in along the edges of the opening. An experienced buck will be reluctant to cross the opening and is likely to pass right in front of you as he moves toward the downwind side to scent-check the decoy.

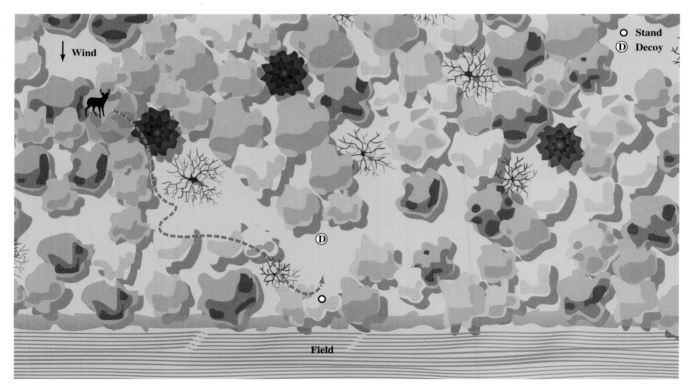

BARRIERS, such as fields, cliffs or lakes, offer another good decoy setup. With your back against the barrier, position the decoy in front of you, in open woods or at the edge of brush. Ideally, you should be downwind of the decoy. When a buck spots the decoy and circles downwind to investigate it, he'll walk between you and the decoy.

Special Situations

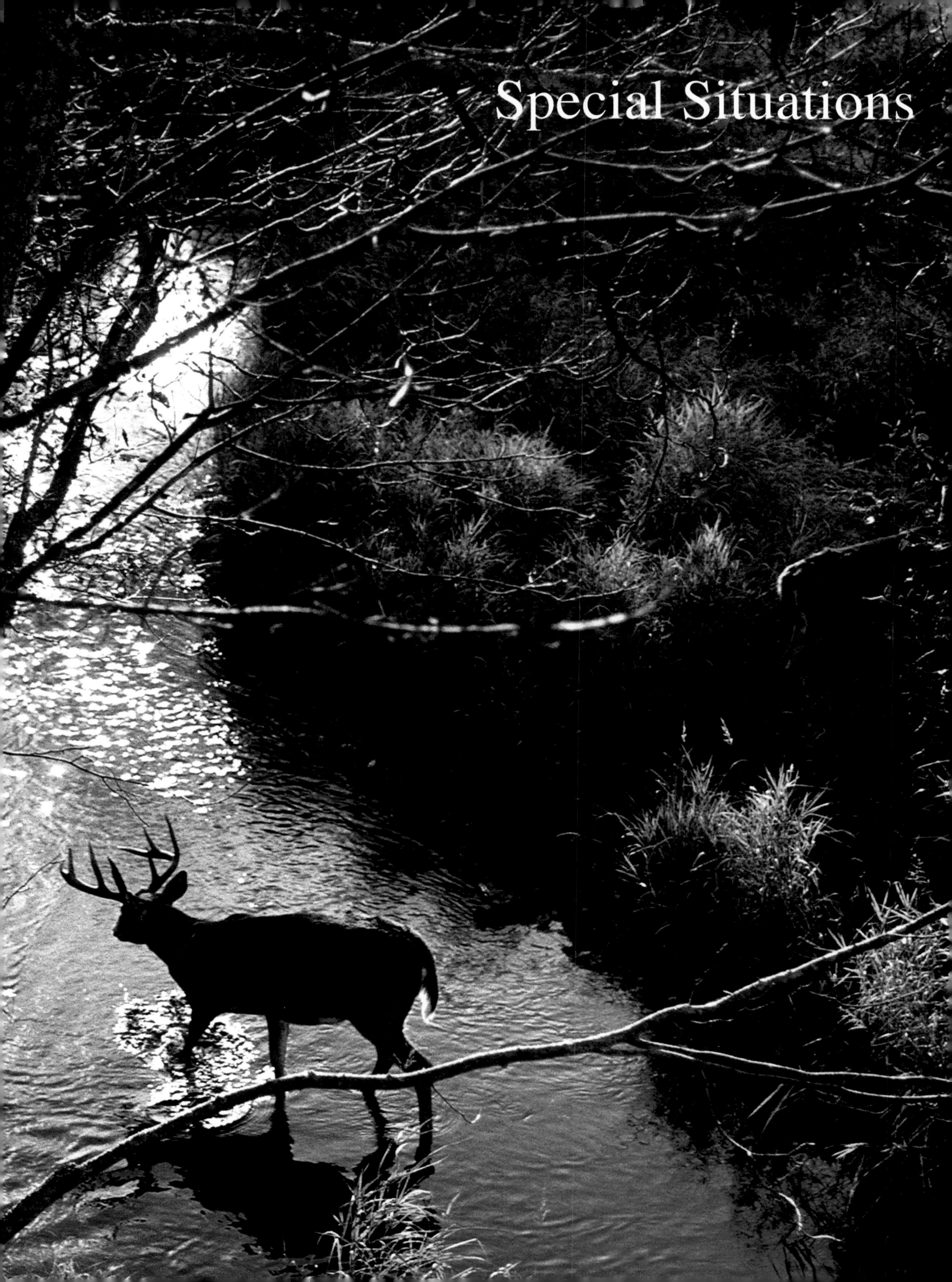

Bedding Areas

I f there's one place in your house where you feel the most secure, it's probably your bedroom. Doors locked, dog on guard, smoke alarm charged, lights out. You're safe and snug in your bed; let down your guard and sleep.

Whitetails never relax in this way. Although they do bed down every day, usually in places just as safe as your own bedroom, they rarely sleep, and they never let down their guard. That's what makes hunting whitetails' bedding areas so frustrating: during most of the legal hunting hours when deer are in their bedrooms, they're on maximum alert, dozing with one eye, two ears and two nostrils open. And to compound the problem, whitetails often use several bedding sites, making it nearly impossible for you to guess which one they're using at any given time. One study uncovered a doe with seventeen different bedding sites throughout her home range. How do you win against odds like that?

Hunting beds is indeed difficult and this is one of the reasons you should employ the technique as a last-ditch effort. If you roust a buck from his bed, your alarmed quarry might abandon its sanctuary and flee to quieter surroundings, perhaps in an area you can't hunt or won't even be able to find. This is why experienced hunters usually work the edges of bedding areas, hoping to ambush a wary buck without spooking him out of the country.

But if the hunting season is just about over and other approaches haven't worked, and if you know precisely where the buck of your dreams will hole up for the day, a direct attack might be the last viable option. But plan and execute your hunt flawlessly, because it probably will be the last chance you get.

AGRICULTURAL LANDS often have limited amounts of dense bedding cover (marked X in the above aerial photograph). As a result, a hunter can pinpoint a buck's preferred bedding location and successfully ambush him from well-placed stands.

Whitetail Bedding Behavior

Understanding how bedded deer behave is essential if you want to hunt them successfully.

After early-morning feeding, bucks usually slip into their beds, although the precise schedule can vary. In lightly hunted areas, for example, bucks generally bed down about an hour after sunrise, but in heavily hunted areas, bucks often become nocturnal, returning to their bedding areas while it's still dark. During the rut, a buck may be late returning to his bed, or might follow a doe to her bedding area.

Once in his bedding area, a buck usually lies down immediately. After he beds down, the buck behaves much like a dairy cow, flicking flies off his ears, licking his coat, regurgitating and chewing his cud from the morning feed. A buck may doze, even while chewing, but rarely sleeps for more than a few minutes.

Every few hours the buck rises to stretch, urinate and maybe browse a bit before bedding down again, sometimes in the same spot, but usually a short distance away. This habit of having many different beds in the same area may benefit the buck by discouraging parasites and by preventing predators from pinpointing his exact location.

Comparing Bed Length to Deer Body Weight

40 inches = 125 pounds

45 inches = 175 pounds

50 inches = 225 pounds

Bed length can be used to identify the bedding area of a large buck. In areas where mature bucks weigh an average of 225 pounds, their beds measure about 50 inches long. Elsewhere, mature bucks weighing 125 to 175 pounds have beds from 40 to 45 inches in length.

Identifying Good Bedding Areas

Deer will bed in any dense cover, but not every such area provides good hunting. Areas with large expanses of heavy cover, 10 acres or more in size, are difficult to hunt, because your buck may be bedded nearly anywhere and can relocate whenever he chooses.

Look instead for habitat with small, isolated areas of secure cover, where a buck's choices are limited. Islands of weeds and brush surrounded by farm fields are prime whitetail bedding sites, as are small brushy wood lots, thickets bordering a river, islands and weedy, abandoned farmyards. In hilly forests, bucks often bed just under the crests of ridges, where they can not only sense danger coming uphill, but can jump down the opposite slope to escape.

When scouting for bedding sign in a promising area, take pains not to spook deer and chase them from the area altogether. Early spring, before green-up, is a good time to locate bedding sites, since deer sign will still be clearly visible in dead leaves and grass, and the deer will have the spring and summer to recover from your intrusion.

To locate bedding sites, backtrack along trails leading from feeding areas and watch ahead for areas of dense cover. Because deer veer off trails singly and in small groups, the game trail will gradually trickle out.

As you progress, check heavy cover areas bordering the trail, searching each spot for droppings and the flattened depressions that show where deer have bedded down.

Although you can't determine the antler size of a deer from studying its bed, you usually can distinguish a buck bedding area from a doe bedroom. If you come upon an area with a scattering of uniformly large beds, it's your lucky day. You have found the haunt of a large-bodied buck, which in all likelihood will have a respectable rack. Look for rubs, scrapes and large tracks to confirm your hunch.

In contrast, bedding areas used by doe and fawn groups have beds and tracks of several different sizes. Don't ignore these areas. Hunt these spots during the rut, and you'll be surprised at the number of bucks wandering through, looking for mates. Hunting doe bedding areas isn't as risky as hunting buck bedrooms, either, because if you spook the females, you haven't necessarily spooked the buck out of the area.

Double-check these scouted sites just before you hunt to make sure they're still in use. Whenever you enter a bedding area, leave as little scent as possible. Get in and out quickly and quietly. Bad weather is a good time to scout, because the wind and rain will cover your scent and sound.

APPROACH a tree stand in the dark, before deer return to the bedding area after feeding.

RATTLING may tempt a bedded buck into shooting range, especially during the rut or the two weeks preceding it.

How to Hunt Bedding Areas

Hunt whitetails in their bedding areas only near the end of the season or when you're after a nocturnal buck that refuses to show itself in daylight. Early in the season, known bedding areas should be left alone to help ensure that deer remain in your hunting territory.

Stand-hunting is the most effective method for hunting bedding areas, because you'll have plenty of heavy cover to hide your presence. Exactly how you stand-hunt a bedding area depends on its size and your dedication.

In smaller bedding areas, you'll have to enter the cover in the morning darkness, at least an hour before the residents are expected home (above). And once you're in these tight spots, you can't leave until an hour after dark. It's common for a bowhunter in a tree stand to observe a buck all day and never get a shot. Be prepared with warm clothing, food, drink, a urine bottle and plenty of patience.

In larger bedding areas, where it may be possible to slip in and out without alerting deer, you can hunt the prime morning and evening hours when deer are coming and going, and leave the bedding area for midday.

Erecting a tree stand in an active bedding zone isn't easy. The best approach is to hang it far in advance

of the hunting season. Where that isn't possible, slip in at night from the direction you least expect the buck to travel, and hang it quietly. Then either climb aboard and wait, or let the stand "settle" for several days before using it.

Whenever erecting a stand, observe strict odor control (p. 104) and avoid disturbing vegetation. The tiniest change in the surroundings can alert an experienced buck. Odor control is essential, because breezes can switch through every degree of the compass during the course of a day. One whiff of your scent and a buck will avoid the area for weeks. An experienced buck might pack up and move out just from the smell of your boots on the ground.

Nasty weather is perfect for hunting dense bedding areas, because heavy rain, snow and wind help cover your scent and noise. Bad weather also discourages deer from moving out to feed in the open, forcing them to do more browsing within the bedding cover.

Bucks near and during the rut often consider their bedding areas to be private turf. They'll readily respond to the sound of an intruding buck, so rattling (above) and calling work well. Because bedded bucks may be close, rattle softly and sparingly, no more than one short session each hour.

Hunting a whitetail buck in his bedroom is a challenging technique, requiring a hunter with considerable discipline and patience. It can also provide some of the most exciting hunting you'll see.

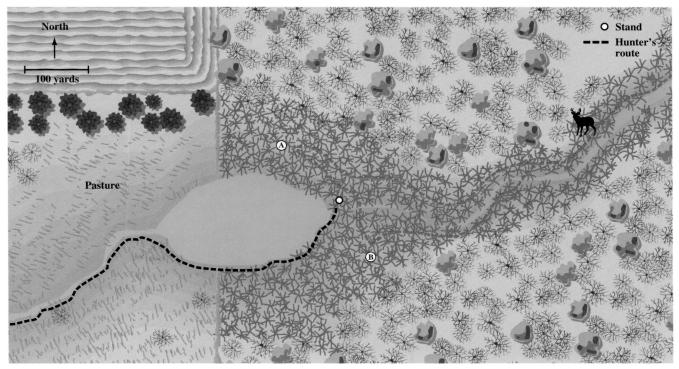

LARGE BEDDING AREAS, such as the thicket shown in this example, can be entered and exited without alarming a bedded buck if a hunter moves very carefully. The hunter must wait for a steady east wind and enter along the creek in the pasture. A buck rising from his bed to browse may move between bedding sites A and B, offering a shot as he crosses the creek.

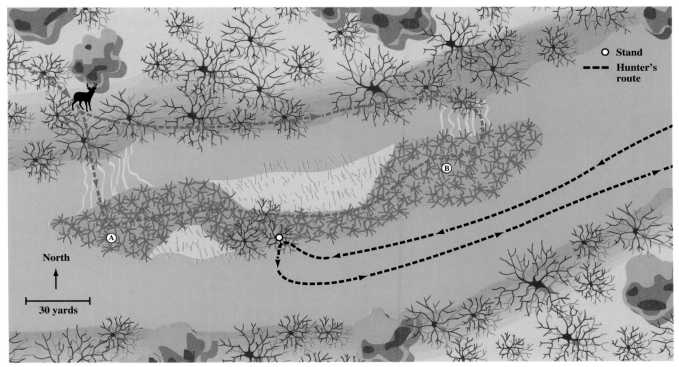

SMALL BEDDING AREAS, such as the island shown in the example above, cannot be entered and exited without alarming the resident buck. A hunter must wait for a steady north wind, then have a partner drop him off by boat downwind of the stand about an hour before sunrise, and remain there until an hour after sunset. During any time of day, the buck may move between bedding sites A and B, offering a close shot.

Scrapes

Scrapes are to whitetail bucks what the golden arches are to McDonald's – big, bold, obvious advertisements. Although hunters have always noticed these oval-shaped patches of bare dirt scratched into the forest floor, it's only in the past few decades that scientific research has recognized these scrapes as visual and olfactory signposts created by bucks to declare their social status and to advertise their breeding readiness to females. The females, for their part, signal their availability by marking the scrapes with their own urine scent.

The significance to hunters is obvious. For a few weeks in fall some of these scrapes are revisited nearly every day, not only by the buck that made them, but by other bucks in the area as well. Finding a scrape is a good sign, but don't make a down payment to your taxidermist just yet. Plenty can go wrong. First, only 20 to 30 percent of a buck's visits to his scrape sites will come during legal shooting hours. Second, a mature buck might have 50 to 200 scrapes scattered across many miles of territory – choosing the right ambush spot can be complicated, to say the least. Finally, bucks tend to be wary when approaching scrapes, sometimes circling out of view to scent-check them from downwind. If they catch a whiff of human odor, they may never again visit the site during daylight hours.

Despite these difficulties, scrape-hunting, done correctly, can be one of the most successful tactics for hunting big bucks.

Scrape Types

Scrapes can be divided into two types: *active scrapes* (also called *breeding scrapes* or *hot scrapes*), which are revisited regularly by bucks; and *nonactive scrapes,* which are not revisited.

Active scrapes are always found under an overhead branch hanging 4 to 5 feet above the ground. After scratching away debris down to bare soil in an oblong area roughly 2 feet by 3 feet, the buck reaches up with his antlers and forehead to break the hanging branch tips and rub his scent on them. Then, he usually chews a broken branch tip and rubs his preorbital gland on it. Finally, he urinates over his tarsal glands and into the scrape, and sometimes defecates in it, too. The buck will regularly return to the scrape site to check for the scent of a doe in estrus and to freshen it with his own scent.

OVERHEAD BRANCHES are as important as the scrape itself. Scientists don't know exactly why bucks chew and rub the branches overhanging scrape sites, but some believe the buck is leaving scent to communicate its social status to other bucks.

Frequency of Scraping and Rubbing Activity by Age Class of Bucks

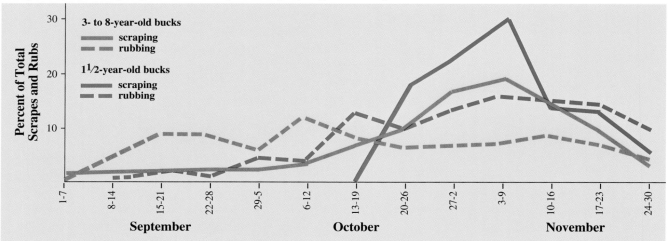

RESEARCH conducted in Michigan's upper peninsula (Ozoga and Verme, 1985) found that 3- to 8-year-old bucks begin scraping and rubbing earlier than 1½-year-old bucks. For both groups, scraping reached its maximum level during November 3 to 9, about 14 days before the peak week of breeding – November 17 to 23.

Nonactive scrapes include random scrapes made by 1½-year-old bucks wandering to and from feeding areas or dispersing from the mother's territory to establish a new home range. These scrapes may or may not have an overhead branch. Another type of nonactive scrape, referred to by some hunters as an *estrus-response scrape,* occurs when a buck hastily scrapes in the spot where a doe has urinated. These scrapes are small in diameter and have no overhead branch.

Some nonactive scrapes begin as active scrapes, but fall into neglect for one of several reasons. Once a buck finds a ready doe, he no longer checks his scrapes. Hunting pressure or a change in the buck's travel habits can also cause him to abandon certain scrapes.

Scrape-Hunting Basics

Scrape-hunting is likely to be successful in areas with good numbers of mature bucks and buck-to-doe ratios of 1:2 or 1:3. The technique is less productive in areas where there are many more females than males; if bucks have no trouble finding mates, they feel no need to advertise by scraping.

Bucks may scrape at any time from August through January, but the activity generally peaks two weeks before the peak breeding time (above), a date which state game departments can provide. Bucks scrape most aggressively when fall temperatures are average or slightly below average. In unusually warm weather, when deer movement in general decreases, bucks are less likely to visit their scrapes.

Bucks may check scrapes at any time of day, but as research conducted through Southwest Missouri State University (Woods and Robbins, 1986) suggests, there are three peak visitation periods. The strongest peak was from 8:45 A.M. to 10:15 A.M.; the second strongest, from 3:45 P.M. to 5:15 P.M.; and the least intense peak, from 11:45 A.M. to 1:15 P.M.

How to Scrape-Hunt

The techniques for hunting scrapes are exactly the same as those for stand-hunting. The most difficult and important part of scrape-hunting is locating scrapes and choosing the right location for your

COMMUNITY SCRAPES, which may measure 6 to 10 feet in diameter, are created by several bucks using the same scrape.

Mock Scrapes

It's possible to draw bucks to a specific area by creating a mock scrape. An imitation scrape that looks and smells authentic can inspire resident bucks to start checking and freshening the site. And before you know it, your mock scrape becomes the real thing.

There are several situations where it makes sense to create a mock scrape: 1) if there are no genuine scrapes anywhere in the area; 2) when you wish to lure a buck into a designated hunting location; or 3) when you want to "speed up" the rut and fool bucks into real scrape activity several days before it would normally begin.

The best site for your mock scrape is one that bucks will be sure to find. A mock scrape placed near an active deer trail or preferred food source, for instance, is more likely to be successful than one placed in remote, thick cover. If you can choose a site that is also convenient for stand-hunting, so much the better.

You will, of course, need a low-hanging branch. Can't find one where you need it? Then use pruning shears to cut a branch with tips ¼ to ¾ inch thick, and tie it with twine about 4 or 5 feet above the ground. The branch must be fresh, not dead. A genuine overhead branch from another scrape is ideal, because it will be prescented.

With a sharp stick or rock, scratch away all vegetation down to bare dirt in a 30-inch circle directly under the tips of the overhead branch. Pour doe-in-estrus lure or buck urine into the scrape. Some hunters pour the scent into a small bottle with holes punched in the cap and bury it just below the surface; others hang a commercial drip bottle well above the scrape so it drips a steady supply of fresh scent onto the ground (p. 103). Finish the mock scrape by dripping forehead-gland scent onto the overhead branch. Freshen the scent often, but if you don't get results within a few days, choose a new location.

MOCK SCRAPE EQUIPMENT includes (1) rubber boots, (2) twine, (3) scent, (4) scent dripper, (5) rubber gloves and (6) pruning shears.

How to Make a Mock Scrape

USE twine to tie the overhead branch 4 to 5 feet off the ground. Wear rubber gloves to avoid leaving your scent on the branch.

SCRATCH out a 30-inch circle and be careful not to kneel in the scrape. Wear rubber boots to avoid leaving your odor on the ground.

DRIP doe-in-estrus or buck-urine scent into the scrape, and forehead-gland scent onto the overhead branch.

stand. Scouting is all-important when it comes to scrape-hunting.

Begin looking for scrapes along predictable travel routes: the border between woods and a feed field or clear-cut, a line of trees bordering a narrow watercourse, the junction of two or more trails, a fenceline or a heavily traveled ridgetop. Keep an eye out for rubbed trees and battered saplings. As a buck gets closer to the rut and becomes more frustrated, he'll rub and fight vegetation with increasing violence, leaving signs that a scrape is probably nearby.

Once you've found one scrape, look for more. Areas with multiple scrapes will provide much better hunting than an area with a single isolated scrape. Perhaps the best hunting opportunities exist along scrape lines – travel routes dotted with three to twelve or more scrapes. To unravel a buck's travel pattern, scout along these scrape lines in both directions until it becomes apparent where the buck beds, and where he goes during his nightly travel routine. To determine which direction the buck travels, study the scrapes carefully; bucks always throw dirt backward when scraping. Fresh tracks can also show you which direction he moves.

Once you've identified a buck's travel pattern by scouting for his scrapes, rubs, tracks and beds, you still must pinpoint which scrapes the buck is most likely to visit during legal shooting hours. This varies from early to late fall. In early fall, only those scrapes near the buck's bedding area will be visited during legal shooting hours. Later, when scraping intensifies, bucks are active throughout the day and may be intercepted far from their bedding areas. The most productive hunting will be in areas where scrapes are concentrated along doe-fawn paths leading between bedding and feeding areas.

Select a stand location as far from the buck's path as possible, given the type of terrain and cover, and the limitations of your weapon. To reduce the chances for spooking approaching bucks, be cautious when erecting, entering and leaving the site (p. 30). Your best opportunity is usually the first time you hunt a particular stand, because the deer haven't had the chance to pattern you.

Because bucks are so active and aggressive during the scraping period, this is an excellent time to use rattling, calling and decoying techniques. Don't be afraid to rattle aggressively – this is the fight season, after all.

Scrape-hunting is trophy hunting at its best. It is one of the few hunting methods that allow you to pursue a specific buck, one-on-one. And nothing is more satisfying than beating a big buck at his own game.

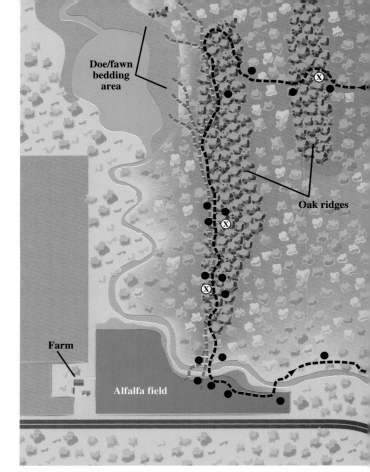

THE TROPHY BUCK featured in this illustration leaves his mid-fall bedding location (A) in late afternoon, travels many miles along oak ridges and alfalfa fields during the night, and finally returns to his bed (B) just after sunrise. Although many of the buck's scrapes (●) are freshened every 24 hours, only those revisited around sunrise and sunset can be hunted successfully.

Based on light hunting pressure, ideal evening stands are marked Ⓔ; morning stands, Ⓜ. The oak ridge to the east, even though it is close to the buck's bedding area, is a poor location for a stand because this ridge is not visited by females, and the buck will soon alter his route and avoid the area. An evening stand placed on the edge of the alfalfa field to the northeast, farther along the buck's route, is also a poor choice, because it will be dark by the time the buck arrives there.

Morning stands must be close enough to the bedding area so the buck passes during daylight, but not so close that you will alert the bedded animal when you exit the stand. The alfalfa field near the farm to the west is too far from the buck's bedding area to be an effective morning site, because it is still dark when the buck passes through this area. The only huntable morning stands lie to the east of the field.

Later in the fall, as the breeding period nears, the buck will probably move his bedding location closer to that of one of the doe-fawn groups. Ideal stands for this period, marked Ⓧ, should be located in areas with a concentration of scrapes and along the buck's travel route between the doe families. Since the buck may revisit these scrapes during any time of the day, these stands can be successfully hunted from sunrise through sunset.

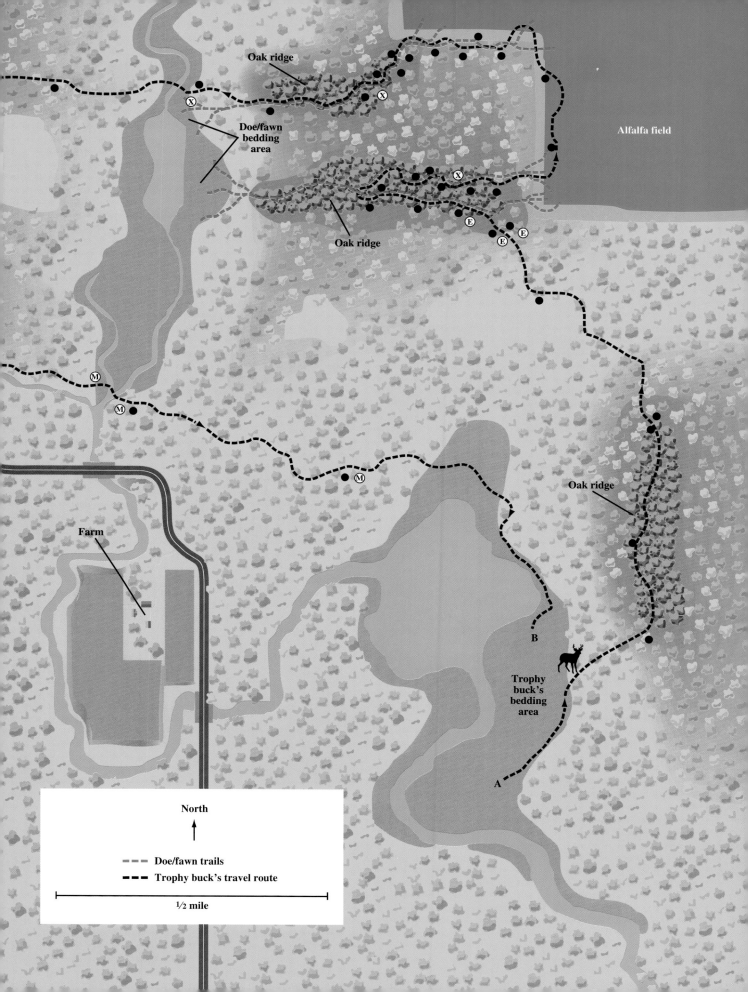

Oak ridge

Ⓧ

Doe/fawn
bedding
area

Alfalfa field

Ⓧ

Oak ridge

Ⓧ

Ⓔ

Ⓔ Ⓔ

Ⓜ

Ⓜ ●

Oak ridge

Ⓜ

Farm

B

Trophy
buck's
bedding
area

A

North

↑

- - - Doe/fawn trails

━ ━ ━ Trophy buck's travel route

½ mile

Cornfields

Across vast sections of the country, modern agriculture has created conditions for an unusual, productive and wildly exciting whitetail hunting tactic – stalking deer in standing corn. Whitetails bedded in the middle of the day are almost impossible to approach in most dense cover. You can drive cornfields, of course (p. 36), but under the right conditions, a single hunter stalking a buck bedded in standing corn can get close enough to hear him chewing his cud.

Cornfield-Hunting Basics

Naturally, this tactic requires specific conditions. First, of course, you need standing corn, which is plentiful in most of the Midwest and much of the irrigated South and West. Isolated fields far from decent woodland bedding cover usually are more productive than vast acres of corn, because deer will be more concentrated in the isolated fields. In big corn country, hunting improves after about 75 percent of standing corn has been harvested and deer are concentrated in remaining fields.

The second requirement is wind and lots of it. Wind usually is a hindrance to deer hunters, but when hunting cornfields, a stiff wind rattling the dry leaves is essential for covering your approach. Without it, you'll be as obvious as an elephant in Rice Krispies. Rain, melting frost and heavy snow can also dampen the noise you make moving through the corn, but wind is best. A constant breeze also blows away any worries about shifting scent.

Though not essential, snow can be an aid to finding bedded bucks in corn. With new snow on the ground you can more easily see fresh tracks and spot deer from a distance.

Before hunting any field you must get permission from the farmer, who may not appreciate unknown predators stomping through his unharvested crops. Explain your technique and reassure him that you'll be hunting slowly and won't be trampling cornstalks. Because deer often damage crops, many farmers welcome skilled hunters who can remove some of the four-legged raiders (below).

Trophy buck feeding in standing corn

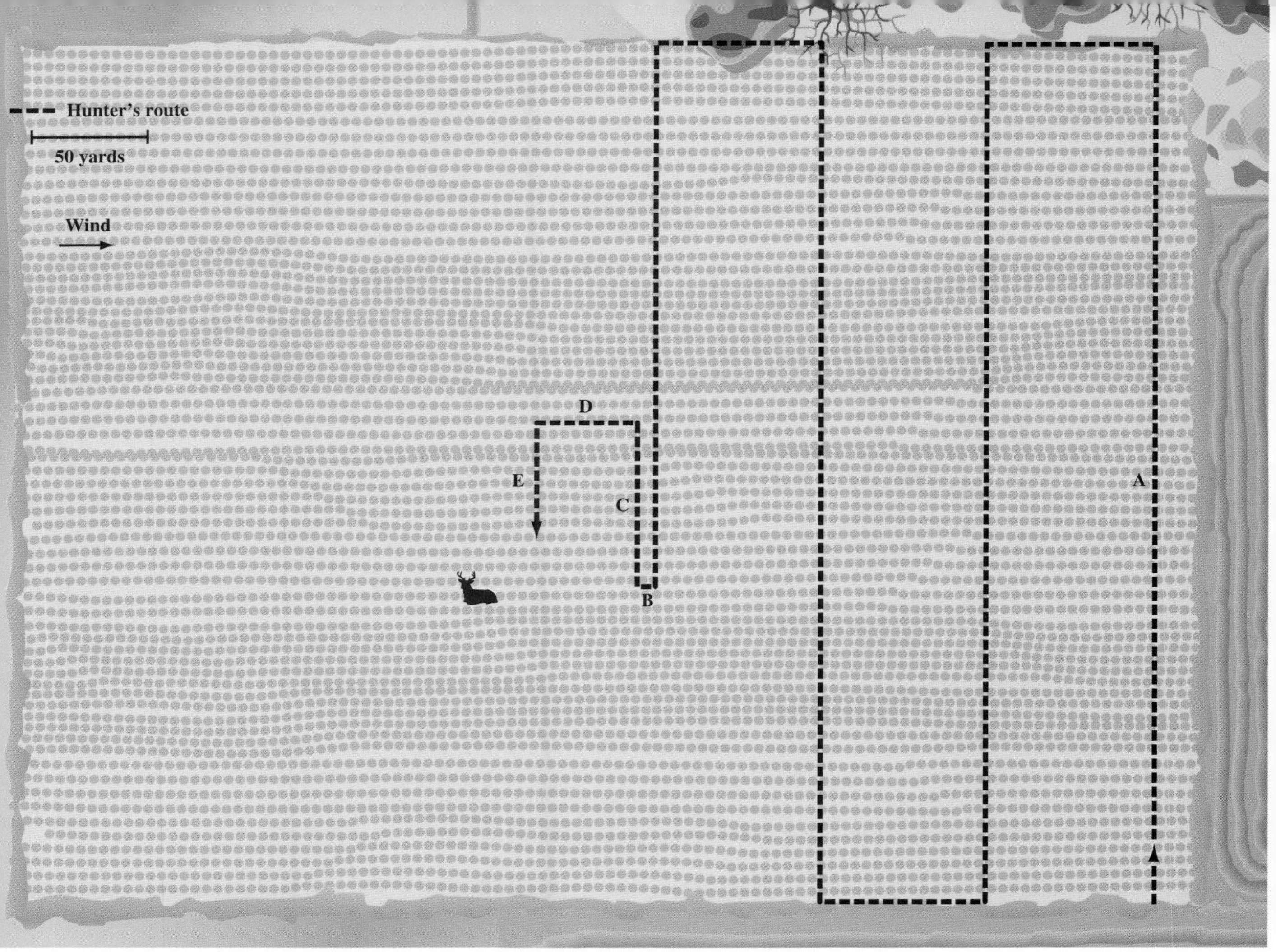

How to Hunt Cornfields

The game is best played during the midday hours between 10:00 A.M. and 3:00 P.M., when deer are bedded. With your eyes and ears on full alert, sneak along the downwind end of the field (A, diagram above), peeking down each row before moving forward to view the next row. Move very slowly and quietly, holding your bow or gun against your chest in a vertical position so the weapon doesn't catch on cornstalks as you cross the rows.

After you've reached the far edge of the field, hike down as far as you can see within the rows – 40 to 100 yards, depending on the density of corn leaves and ground weeds. Now cut back across the rows in the opposite direction, again peeking down the rows for deer.

Continue this back and forth pattern until you've covered the field – or until you spot your buck. As

you traverse the field, try not to walk over the crest of hills where deer may spot your silhouette against the sky.

If something catches your eye, check it with binoculars. Weeds, dirt clods, and rocks can look like bedded deer, and bedded deer, because they don't move much, can look like rocks. Be sure to look ahead across the rows in case there is something right in your path.

After you identify a buck (B), you can take the shot immediately, if the deer is within range, or you can stalk closer.

Before beginning your stalk, quickly use binoculars to check for other deer that may be bedded nearby. Spooking a hidden deer can ruin your stalk. Now, estimate the buck's distance from you. Next, backtrack 10 to 15 rows (C) – the idea is to put enough standing corn between you and the deer to block his view.

Now take a deep breath, because here comes the adrenaline rush. Slowly sneak down the row (D), moving so you'll be within shooting range when you

JUMPED DEER often circle downwind to check your scent. Stand and watch, ready to shoot as the buck crosses the row in which you are standing (A). If the shot is too far or the buck passes through the row too quickly, wait for him to approach closer (B); you may need to crouch low to find a clear shooting lane across the rows of corn.

move back toward the row holding your buck. For a bowhunter, this distance is usually within 10 to 20 yards of the deer; for a gun hunter, slightly farther.

Now the hard part. You must sneak back across the intervening rows (E), again checking for hidden deer (right) and losing your own protective cover as you go. Watch carefully for your target, and when you see it, move as needed to get a clear shot. You can usually shoot across two or three intervening rows of corn. Don't attempt to get into the same row as the buck unless there's no other way. Take your time and make the shot count.

That's all there is to hunting cornfields. The strategy isn't complicated – it just provides nerve-racking thrills in conditions where other hunting strategies are useless.

Tools of the Trade

BOWHUNTERS often shoot at very close range — peep sights and pins are superfluous. Practice shooting instinctively at 20 yards or less with a bow that draws quickly and quietly — recurves and long bows are best. Ideal camouflage patterns have a light brown background with darker-colored angled lines, mimicking the pattern of cornstalks and leaves.

GUN HUNTERS also need quick-handling weapons. Open sights are usually sufficient. Scopes, if used at all, should be low-powered, no more than 4×. There is no need for lightning bullet speed and long-range ballistic performance for this style of hunting. Shotguns with short slug barrels are easy to handle in standing corn; and because slugs don't fly far, shotguns are safer than rifles.

Cattails

Cattails grow in mud and shallow water, are difficult and noisy to walk through, impossible to see through and just plain irritating when their downy seeds waft up your nose and into your eyes. We'd recommend you stay out of them entirely, except for one small fact: cattail sloughs and marshes often are brimming with whitetail bucks.

If you could ask them, whitetails might admit they'd just as soon live elsewhere, too, but they know that sloughs and swamps filled with cattails and other reeds are safe havens. Those few predators with the determination to plow through these tough reeds make so much noise that deer have plenty of time to hide or sneak away. Cattail marshes are giant sanctuaries, and as the hunting season progresses, whitetails pile into them to escape hunting pressure. In some marshes, bucks are so seldom bothered by hunters that they boldly chase females in broad daylight.

Many large cattail marshes are state-owned lands open to public hunting. If you have difficulty getting permission to hunt on private land, hunting cattails may be your best chance at tagging a trophy buck.

Cattail-Hunting Basics

Four factors determine how eagerly deer use cattails. First is the size of the cover. The larger the marsh or slough, the more attractive it is, because deer can wander far into its depths where they're seldom disturbed and rarely taken by hunters. In large cattail marshes, bucks can play cat-and-mouse with hunters all day, every day, and never get tagged.

The second factor is the quantity of thick bedding cover in the surrounding area. If deer are hiding successfully in brush and woods, they don't need to

Cattail marsh after a winter ice storm

Hunter examining an aerial photo of cattails bordering a large river

seek shelter in cattails. But if cattails are the only cover available, as is the case in prairie pothole country, they become vital to whitetails.

The third factor is the amount of dry ground within the marsh. Deer swim readily and don't mind wet feet, but they aren't going to lie in water all day. Sloughs choked with cattails but essentially dry are attractive to whitetails. A few inches of water doesn't necessarily preclude use, because deer often can press down enough dead cattails to create a fairly dry bed. Deep-water cattail marshes can also hold whitetails, but only if they are studded with dry islands.

Finally, hunting pressure affects how whitetails use cattails. When hunters are crawling through woods and uplands, deer seek peace in undisturbed reed beds. They remember these areas from year to year, and use them as giant sanctuaries whenever hunting pressure grows intense.

Although cattails are used by deer year-round, they become particularly important in late fall and winter, when standing corn has been harvested and other cover is at a premium. Thick stands of head-high reeds provide perfect bedding cover during winter storms and bitter winds (above, left).

Scouting Cattails

At first glance, a big marsh choked with cattails looks like a mass of dense, impenetrable cover that could harbor deer almost anywhere. On closer inspection, you'll find that most deer travel is concentrated on well-defined trails leading between high-ground bedding islands and a few grassy openings in the marsh. Most of the cattails are just too difficult to push through, so deer keep to the established trails and bedding areas, except in emergencies.

Deer sometimes cross high water, but their trails are usually found on

SMALL BOATS are ideal for locating and hunting cattail islands before the water freezes. Paddle or push-pole your boat, approaching islands from downwind, where you'll raise the least suspicion.

berms, old roads or through areas with shallow water and a firm bottom.

Open spaces on relatively dry ground are popular whitetail rutting centers. Typically, these are ringed with phragmites and carpeted in short slough grass. Bucks patrol these areas throughout the day and often bed on their edges while watching for females.

Islands or humps of dry ground are popular bedding sites and are often marked with red osier dogwood shrubs, Russian olives, willows, cottonwoods and sometimes cedars. In some marshes, dry ground is tougher to locate because it is marked only with phragmites or low slough grass. Find these spots by viewing the marsh from a high vantage, such as a bordering tree, bluff or barn roof.

Watch for lines of trees that indicate old roads or water-control berms; deer prefer these dry trails over mucky ones. Mark the obvious trails, bedding areas, openings and deep water on a hand-drawn map. If possible, take compass or GPS readings, because features will be nearly impossible to see once you're inside the cattails.

If you can't get a bird's-eye view of the marsh, check for aerial photos (opposite page) with the Aerial Photography Field Office (p. 10). The best way to view the marsh is by renting a small plane and taking your own photographs. From a low altitude, you'll be able to spot all the main deer trails and bedding islands.

Finally, slip on hip boots and go exploring. Do this scouting well before hunting season begins, so deer have a chance to recover from your intrusion. Deer trails emerging from cattails are easy to follow and can be explored on foot. In deep marshes, you might need a canoe or small boat (above) to reach bedding islands. Try to keep your bearings by compass or GPS, and maintain a map as you go, marking each fork in the trail. Some hunters strategically mark the trail with slim poles and reflecting tape.

A good working knowledge of deer movement in cattails makes hunting much easier. All you have to do is determine the best travel lanes, match your schedule to the deer's, and arrange a meeting.

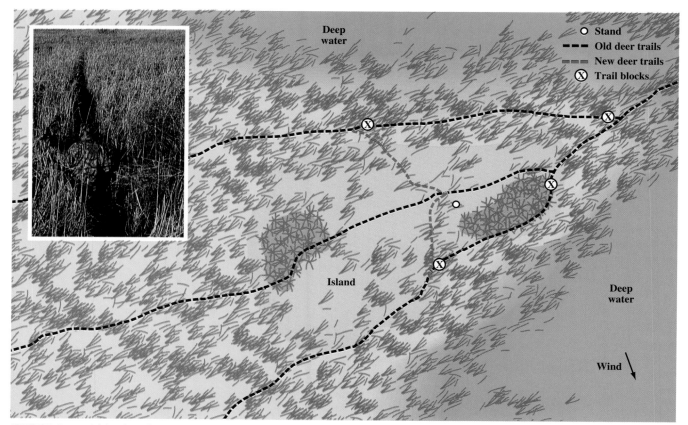

Legend:
- ○ Stand
- ‐ ‐ ‐ Old deer trails
- ‐ ‐ ‐ New deer trails
- ⓧ Trail blocks

Deep water

Deep water

Island

Wind

GUIDE deer within shooting range of your blind by tramping down new trails (inset) and blocking old trails with cut-off cattails or brush. This technique can be used when there are no good stand locations along natural deer trails. Wait at least a week before hunting, so deer can become accustomed to the new route.

How to Hunt Cattails

Although two or more hunters can successfully drive cattails, stand-hunting from a ground blind is more popular. Once you've identified major bedding areas and trails in the marsh, make a cattail blind (opposite page) where you can intercept bucks as they search for females or move to and from feeding areas. All deer in cattails share the same trails, so you can expect to see many deer, including some of the giants.

When ambushing deer from the ground, remove just enough cattail stalks to clear shooting lanes. Cutting too much vegetation may alert the buck of your dreams and cause him to hold up just short of your carefully opened shooting lane.

Guide deer within shooting range of your blind by tromping down new trails where you need them (above) and blocking old routes with brush or cut-off

cattails shoved into the mud. Do this one or two weeks before you plan to hunt, so the deer have plenty of time to become comfortable with the change in scenery.

Stand-hunting can also be done from a tripod stand (right). When placed properly, a tripod allows gun hunters to look over bedding areas and trail intersections from considerable distances.

As you stand-hunt, observe the usual practices for avoiding detection. Watch the wind. Mask your odor. Arrive at your stand in the dark hours of early morning, long before bucks return from their nighttime travels.

How to Make a Cattail Blind

CUT cattails with a folding saw and carry them to your chosen ground-blind location.

BUILD a semicircular blind by poking the ends of the cattails into the mud. The open side of the blind should face away from the direction you expect to see deer.

BEGIN assembling a *mud stool* by sinking a pole through a flat board and deep into the marshy ground. The board adds stability for the seat.

PLACE the swiveling seat on top of the pole. The mud stool lets you sit comfortably while keeping a low profile.

SUPPORT your bow in an upright, ready position with a Bow-vest® (above) or a forked stick.

WATCH for approaching deer through narrow shooting openings in the blind. An ideal blind is tall and dense enough to hide a sitting hunter.

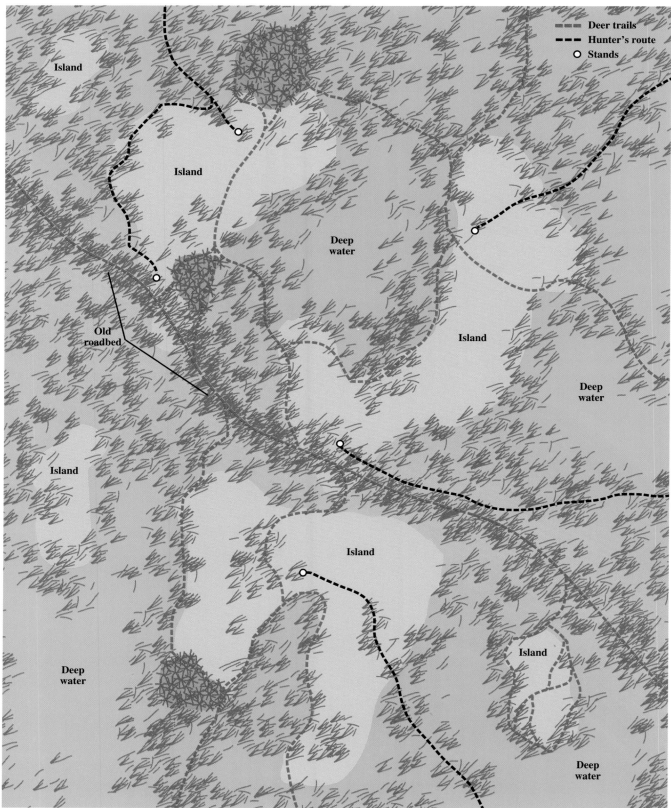

Deer trails
Hunter's route
○ Stands

Island

Island

Deep water

Old roadbed

Island

Deep water

Island

Island

Deep water

Island

Island

Deep water

POSITION your stand where two or more trails meet. Avoid hunting small parcels of high ground; few deer use these areas, and it is difficult to get in and out without being detected. Larger islands make better stand sites. When entering and exiting your stand, choose routes downwind of the deer trail you're hunting.

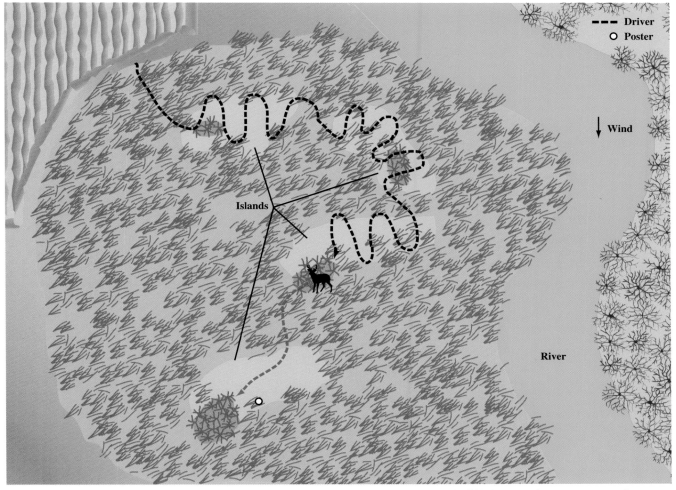

IDENTIFY all areas of high ground where deer bed or feed. Position drivers upwind of high ground areas; posters, downwind. In large marshes, drivers can push deer from island to island, toward posters waiting at the last area of high ground. All members of the drive must adhere to strict safe-shooting zones to avoid accidents.

To avoid crossing trails used by deer, you may need to use a roundabout path when entering your stand. Each time you approach, weave a slightly different route to avoid making an obvious, well-worn trail. This prevents other hunters from discovering your ambush site and reduces the chance that deer will begin using your entrance trail rather than the game trail you've carefully staked out.

In large cattail marshes, a pack frame can be used to quietly haul in gear. You can lighten your daily load by storing decoys, drinking water, food and other gear near your stand, but make sure your supplies are hidden from the noses of deer and the eyes of other hunters.

While most hunters use stand-hunting techniques, others drive cattails (above) with good success. Conduct a cattail drive in much the same way as a pheasant hunt, zigzagging through cover and stop-ping frequently for long intervals to unnerve hiding bucks. Does and fawns usually break first, then small bucks. Monster bucks may hold tight until you nearly step on them.

In small, dense sloughs of no more than 5 acres, it is relatively easy to drive deer out of cover toward posters positioned just outside the cattails. In big marshes, you won't drive deer out of the cattails, but you can move them around inside the marsh. As the drivers foul the air with odor and noise, bucks often sneak to nearby islands – where posters wait in ambush.

Cattail marshes offer some the worst of all possible hunting conditions, but they also promise huge rewards. A hunter with the skill and stamina to brave the cattails may discover trophy bucks in surprising numbers. All the exertion and discomfort will make your reward that much sweeter.

Bucks under Pressure

One of the most difficult challenges for a white-tail hunter is tagging a big buck in territory that sees throngs of gun hunters each and every season. Because the yearly whitetail harvest is so heavy in these areas, it's a rare buck who lives long enough to reach trophy size. And under this intense hunting pressure, surviving deer quickly learn to move their bedding sites to the densest, most impenetrable cover around, or to out-of-the-way pockets where hunters rarely go. A wily old buck who has survived several seasons of this kind of pressure has probably learned to spend the daylight hours bedded down and hidden in areas virtually inaccessible to hunters.

High-pressure hunting areas include most farmlands and rural habitat near cities and towns, since these areas are the only option for urban-dwelling hunters who don't have the time or money to travel to better hunting grounds. In any region, whitetail habitat with flat, easy-to-hike terrain sees considerable hunting pressure, as does any state- or federally-owned land open to public hunting. Hunting pressure is also high in areas with a strong hunting tradition, in regions where firearms seasons are long, or where license sales are unlimited.

Sounds like a hopeless situation? Take heart. Even under these less-than-ideal conditions, a hunter with determination, a comprehensive knowledge of whitetail behavior and a willingness to scout extensively has a better-than-average chance of taking a decent buck.

Hunting Basics

Scout high-pressure habitat well before hunting season opens. Don't worry too much about scrape lines, rubs and deer trails near feed fields, because these signs will mean little in a few weeks when pressured deer are fleeing to deep, heavy cover. Instead, look for dense, impenetrable pockets of brush, cattails, coniferous trees and swampy areas where bucks are likely to hide once the shooting starts. You may need to clear entry and exit paths into this formidable cover, as well as shooting lanes where you expect to see deer. You'll be using standard stand-hunting techniques (p. 23) to hunt these pockets of dense cover.

If the area has no dense cover, deer may move out of the area altogether in search of sanctuaries far from roads. Look for wooded corridors, saddles between valleys, fencelines or river bottoms that deer can use as escape routes when leaving their normal habitat.

An ideal location for a hunting stand is where several escape routes converge near a sanctuary with dense cover. If you can identify such a site for your opening-day stand, relax – the worst is over. In a

few days or weeks, as dozens of eager, competing hunters invade the woods, deer will file past your stand like Christmas shoppers at the local mall.

Once you've identified the best escape routes, locate the most advantageous stand site to cover them. You'll want a good view with plenty of cover behind you to break up your outline. A tree stand can be ideal, especially if it lets you see down into heavy ground cover, but ground stands are usually adequate for gun hunters. Elaborate blinds aren't necessary unless you tend to fidget on stand. Too much cover can interfere with your vision, hearing and shooting. Set up just close enough to the escape route to ensure a good shot. At some stands you may need to clear shooting lanes.

Experienced stand-hunters anticipate the likelihood of shifting winds and wisely prepare two stands for each location, allowing them to stay downwind of approaching deer.

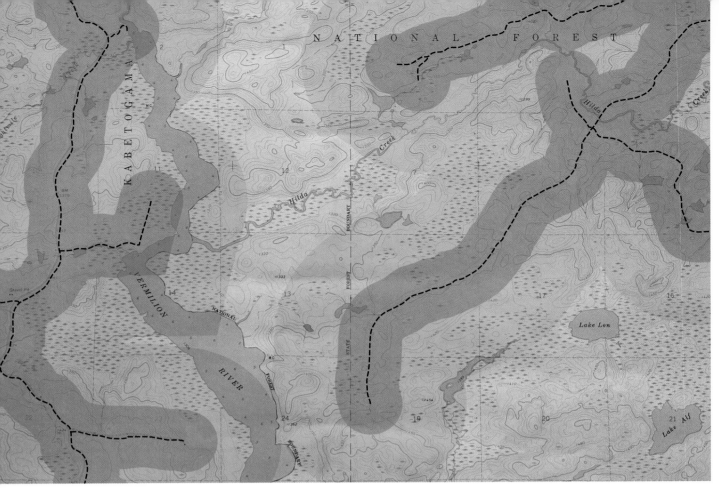

SANCTUARIES are areas that bucks seek out once the shooting starts. With an orange highlighter, shade in the region within 1/4 mile of roads and other access trails; this area will be the most heavily hunted and hold few deer. Use yellow to shade areas 1/4 to 3/4 mile; this land will see moderate hunting pressure, but may hold deer if there are large amounts of thick cover serving as sanctuaries. Areas beyond this shaded habitat will see little hunting pressure and hold the most deer.

How to Hunt Deer under Pressure

On opening morning of firearm season, dress in warm blaze-orange clothing from head to toe. Since you'll be sitting on stand for most of the day, pack a "quiet" lunch with no noisy foil or paper wrappings, and bring along a comfortable seat and a urine bottle. You'll be sitting on stand as long as possible; other hunters will be afield most of the day, driving deer your way.

Slip quietly into your stand well before first light. Approach from downwind and be careful not to leave your scent where deer might detect it. Practicing good odor control (p. 104) and using natural scents around your stand (p. 99) can reassure a jittery deer that it's safe to pass.

Consider wind direction when taking up your stand position, and don't be afraid to move if the wind

shifts during the day. When there is no breeze, remember that scent moves uphill as ground warms up in late morning. In late afternoon, cooling air flows toward low areas, carrying your scent with it.

When the first headlights and slamming truck doors disturb the early morning silence, get ready. Deer are already becoming nervous as the first hunters begin to enter the field, and they'll soon be moving your way.

As you sit and wait, scan the area by slowly rotating your head from side to side, taking 15 to 20 seconds to cover the arc. Few deer will detect these slow movements. Keep your eyes moving, but not too quickly; you're more likely to spot deer if you study the surroundings carefully.

Listen for the sound of hooves, and if you hear a promising noise, slowly turn toward the sound. If you spot a buck, wait until the deer's view of you is blocked, then slowly lift your weapon.

If a buck spots your movement, it will either snort and bolt immediately, or stare intently to evaluate the

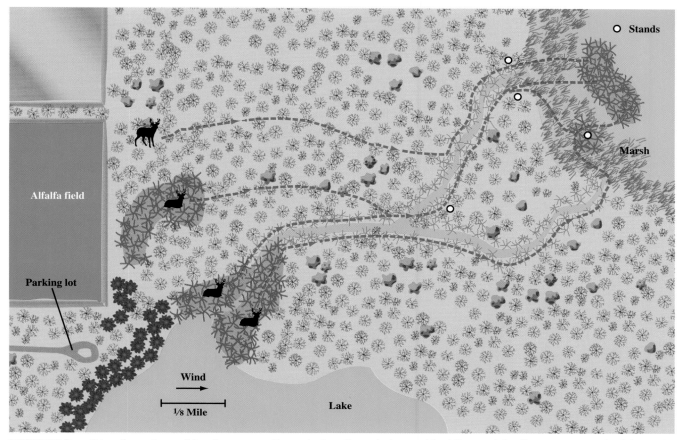

HUNTERS walking from the parking lot eventually push deer from their usual bedding and feeding areas near the lake and the alfalfa field. The animals use the brush along the creek as an escape route when traveling to the island sanctuaries of the marsh. Ideal stand locations stake out these escape routes, taking advantage of the hunting pressure.

motion. If you're a gun hunter, you may still get a shot if you continue raising your weapon slowly into position, avoiding sudden, jerky movements. Fire as soon as the buck is in your gun sight.

If you haven't tagged a buck after a few days of stand-hunting within pockets of dense cover or along an escape route, then look elsewhere for hiding deer. A wise buck can find refuge in the oddest places – in irrigation ditches, in the middle of plowed fields or bedroom-size weed patches, behind farm barns, in backyard orchards or even in brushy ditches along highways.

If you're a gun hunter, try "jump-hunting" these pockets of cover, prepared to shoot quickly at close range. Some hunters in hilly terrain toss rocks into cover to spook holed-up deer into showing themselves. Be patient: big bucks may lie low until you literally step on them.

If all your best efforts fail, it's possible that bucks are hiding on private lands that are off-limits to hunters. You can't trespass on private property, of course, but you can scout the boundaries of these

areas. Look for tracks indicating bucks are using this cover for a daytime bedding sanctuary. If you find such evidence, wait until hunting pressure declines in midweek, then take up an early-morning stand near the private land, where you may be able to ambush the buck as he returns to his bedding site at first light.

As the hunting season progresses, maintain a notebook with sketched maps of locations you've hunted. Note escape routes, bedding sanctuaries and all deer sightings. If you tag a buck or see several in a specific area, hunt the same stand in following seasons. As long as the habitat and hunting pressure remain constant, bucks will use the same escape routes and sanctuaries. Over the course of several years, you'll identify stand sites that are consistently productive and weed out those that aren't.

When you must share a hunting area with many other hunters, make the best of a bad situation. Locate pockets of heavy cover and escape routes leading to deer sanctuaries, set up well in advance and let competing hunters push deer right into your lap.

Fooling the Whitetail's Nose

Using Scents

Cover scents

If you can fool a buck's ears by rattling and calling, and fool his eyes with a decoy, why not fool his nose with scents?

Whitetails don't use elaborate visual signs to signal each other, and they have a pretty limited vocal vocabulary. But they do have an elaborate and sophisticated language based on their acute sense of smell. A doe identifies her fawn by odor, and the fawn can trail its mother by following the interdigital scent she leaves on the ground. A buck marks rubs with scent from his forehead gland (p. 102), and he routinely tracks and finds females in estrus using nothing but his nose. Sense of smell is the most important means of whitetail communication, but, unfortunately, it's the one we least understand.

Smell is said to be the most primal of all senses, and it's easy to imagine primitive hunters anointing themselves with fresh doe urine or the strong odor of deer tarsal glands as they prepared for the hunt. Today, modern hunters have given up wearing skins and living in caves, but each fall, many of us still set out mysterious concoctions of liquids, gels and sprays in an attempt to appease the goddess of the hunt – or to at least lure one of her whitetail bucks within shooting range.

There are hundreds of commercial deer-scent products available to the modern hunter. Sometimes these odoriferous dousings work, sometimes they don't; and hunters are often left scratching their heads at the mystery. What exactly is going on?

The reality is that humans simply can't detect most of the scents deer use to communicate, let alone interpret what they mean. But we suspect that deer are attracted to food odors, are reassured by the scent of deer urine, and that bucks are stimulated by the odor of a doe in estrus. Scent can help you tag a good buck – but only if you pick the right scent and use it in the right place and at the right time.

Choosing and Using Scents

There are four categories of deer scent available: cover scents, food attractor scents, deer urine attractor scents, and gland attractor scents.

Cover scents (above), as the name suggests, are intended to cover up human odors by masking them with a stronger scent. You can choose from a variety of cover odors, including fox or raccoon urine, livestock or deer droppings, natural soil, skunk musk, and aromatic vegetation like pines and cedars. Just how effectively these scents cover up human odor is debatable. Some hunters swear by them; others insist that deer can detect human scent right through the

Food attractor scents

Deer urine attractor scents

most powerful cover scents. We do know that overuse of a single cover scent can teach deer to associate it with hunters, effectively turning it into an alarm scent. For this reason it's best to alternate two or three different cover scents if you're hunting an area for several consecutive days.

Many hunters believe that the best cover scents are natural aromatic odors common in the hunting area, because these seem least suspicious to whitetails. If you hunt pine woods, for example, crush needles against your boots and pants legs, or hang bruised pine branches around your stand. Or, if you hunt pastures, step through fresh livestock dung as you walk.

Hunters who use commercial cover scents sometimes douse the scent on special boot scent pads, or on a drag rag tied with twine to a belt loop. Or, you can place plastic film canisters filled with scent around your stand. When hunting from tree stands, treat the bottom three or four steps with scent to cover any odor deposited when you climb the tree.

Food attractor scents (above) are used to lure deer by appealing to their hunger. Popular food attractor aromas include apple, acorn, sweet corn and persimmon scent. Although they can't lure deer from great distances, these scents can make a whitetail veer from its normal route, stop or loiter long enough to present a good shot.

Hunters can make their own food attractor scents by crushing local forage vegetation, such as alfalfa, corn, apples or peanuts. Place the crushed pulp upwind of your stand in good shooting lanes, but make sure you're not breaking any regulations against baiting game animals.

Deer urine attractor scents (above) come in three main varieties: buck urine, doe urine, and doe-in-estrus urine. Doe-in-estrus scent is by far the most popular product in this category – the magic potion that hunters hope will bring in that big buck. Sometimes, it does exactly that.

Commercially made estrus scent is widely available, but the problem is that no one knows for sure what constitutes a good product. Does it have to be genuine, pure urine from a doe in estrus, or should it be doctored with additional chemicals? Does it need to be fresh, or is the scent just as effective if it's been frozen and stored? And even if these factors are important, the product labels may not tell you if the scent is genuine or doctored. Your best option is to talk with other hunters who have used a variety of products and experiment with their recommendations.

If you're stand-hunting, doe-in-estrus scent can be used both to attract bucks and to cover up your own odor. You can pour it on rags and hang them on branches, sprinkle the scent on the ground, place it

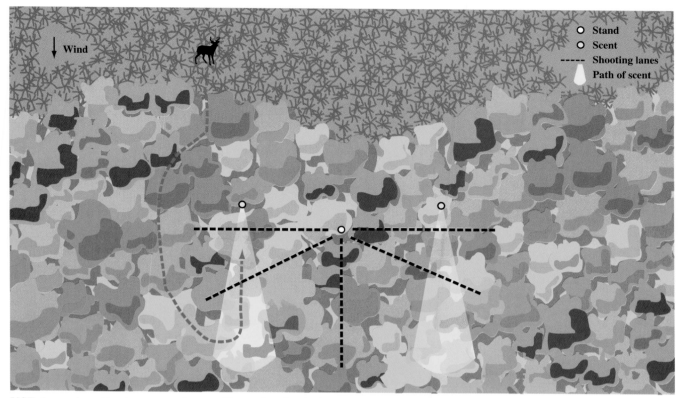

USE deer urine attractor scent when rattling to lure bucks into close shooting range.

in plastic film canisters or even spray it periodically into the air so it drifts on the wind.

We've also seen instances where a hunter who soaks a boot pad or drag rag with estrus scent can lay a trail that brings a buck right to his feet. One of the most effective dragging techniques involves using a fresh tarsal gland taken from a rutting buck (below).

Ordinary buck or doe urine, when used in conjunction with other hunting tactics, can provide just the touch of authenticity needed to bring a buck within

shooting range. When using a decoy, for example, you can make your dummy extra convincing by attaching a urine-scent patch to its hind leg.

When rattling (above), you can short-stop a buck's tendency to circle downwind by placing urine scent 20 to 30 yards to your right and left as you face the breeze. As the buck circles in to scent-check you, he'll hit the urine scent trail first and follow it forward before detecting your human scent. If a buck circles your location and gets downwind, try spraying diluted urine into the air. A buck that detects this

How to Lay a Scent Trail Using a Tarsal Gland

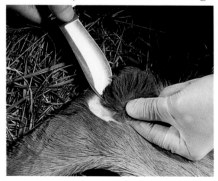

CUT the tarsal gland off a rutting buck. The tarsals are located halfway up the insides of the hind legs.

SATURATE the tarsal gland with doe-in-heat scent, and store the soaked gland in a small plastic bag until you need it.

LEAVE a scent trail to your stand by dragging the gland along the ground with a piece of twine tied to a belt loop.

Whitetail Glands

– by Dr. David Samuel

Location of scent-producing glands

Deer have several external glands, some of which secrete scents called *pheromones,* which serve as signals to other deer. The glands most important to hunters are described below.

The *tarsal glands* are located on the hocks – the inner surfaces of the hind legs. These large glands secrete lipids that interact with urine, producing an odor that probably functions as a sexual attractant or to communicate dominance to other deer. During the rut, when the glands become stained with urine, the tarsals are readily visible. To mark a scrape, the buck rubs these glands together while urinating over them.

The *metatarsal glands* are situated on the outer sides of the lower hind legs. About 1½ inches long, the metatarsals are most prominent in whitetails residing in the North, and are rather indistinct in deer living at southern latitudes. Little is known about their function, but one researcher suggests that the metatarsals may aid in *thermoregulation* – controlling body heat.

The small *interdigital glands*, located between the toes of the hooves, secrete an odor which marks deer trails. Some biologists believe that fawns do not leave interdigital odor, an adaptation that makes it difficult for predators to follow them.

The *preorbital gland*, located in a slit near the inside corner of the eye, has not been studied in whitetails. When studying red deer, however, biologists have noted that this tear duct gland is more prominent in dominant stags than submissive deer, suggesting that the gland serves some social communication function.

The *forehead gland* is located between the eyes and antlers. For years it was assumed that deer rubbing trees used only their antlers, but researchers have recently learned that rutting bucks also mark trees using their forehead glands. Since this behavior is seen most frequently in the most dominant bucks, scientists believe that whitetails use secretions from the forehead gland to mark territory and communicate their dominance to other deer. Trees marked in this way become a focal point for deer interactions. Although females also have forehead glands, they scent-mark much less frequently than do bucks.

Dr. David Samuel (above), a Professor of Wildlife Biology at West Virginia University, is the author of many scientific papers on deer biology. He serves on the board of directors of the Pope and Young Club.

odor may come charging in, convinced you're the real McCoy.

When scrape-hunting, you can use urine scent to freshen a genuine scrape or to give authenticity to a mock scrape you've created. Pour some of the scent in the scrape, or place a saturated cotton ball near the scrape and cover it with debris. You can also hang a scent dripper over a scrape to keep the site fresh (right). A buck scent-checking the scrape from the safety of nearby cover will probably step into the open to get a good sniff – and to provide you with a good shot.

Gland attractor scents (right) are the latest weapons in the olfactory arsenal. Made from the secretions of whitetail tarsal glands, forehead glands, preorbital glands or interdigital glands, these attractor scents are used in much the same way as urine attractor scents. They can be used alone or mixed with urine scents. Like urine attractor scents, gland scents can be used to lay down scent trails or to mask your odor near a stand. Preorbital and forehead gland scents are especially good for luring bucks into visiting scrapes or rubs – either genuine sites, or those created by a hunter (below).

If using scents seems like a mysterious, imprecise art, remember that scent is the language by which

Gland attractor scents

whitetails conduct everyday conversation. With our poor sense of smell, we'll never be able to "hear" this whitetail language, but we can learn how to mimic a few basic messages. Used alone, no scent can guarantee you a successful hunt. But when used properly, in conjunction with other hunting strategies, a scent may well be the siren's call that brings a trophy buck right into your sights.

How to Apply Gland Attractor Scents

Gland attractor scent dripped on mock rub (left) and overhead branch (right)

Odor Control

When it comes to whitetails, the nose knows. A deer might get suspicious if it hears a nylon jacket rasp against a branch; it might stop and stare if it spies a hunter silhouetted against the sky; but when its nostrils catch a whiff of a hunter, that deer is gone.

As far as deer are concerned, humans stink, and it isn't the result of bad personal hygiene. Whitetails simply have incredibly sensitive noses, and to them even the most compulsively clean hunter smells as obvious as a pair of ripe old socks.

That leaves two options: hunt into the wind so deer can't catch your odor, or find some way to eliminate the human odors that deer associate with danger.

For thousands of years, the "hunt into the wind" option was all hunters had, and it worked fine as long as the wind direction remained unchanged. Unfortunately, nature is fickle; breezes swirl and waft and eddy to all points of the compass at the most inopportune times.

ODOR-CONTROL PRODUCTS include: (1) washing machine detergents; (2) clothing and body sprays, powders and wipes; (3) hair and body soaps.

In desperation, hunters tried coating themselves in the fresh skins of their prey or disguising themselves with foul-smelling concoctions – everything from dung to skunk spray. But up until now, whitetails have often smelled through the disguises.

Today, however, thanks to modern science, it's actually possible to reduce your stench enough to fool a deer's powerful sense of smell. The strategy isn't easy, though. Odor control requires the use of specific products in the hands of a hunter willing to be religious about their application.

An absolutely dedicated deer hunter can employ this system to deadly effect. Some hunters practicing disciplined scent control have witnessed trophy bucks crossing downwind within bow range, completely oblivious to the presence of the delighted hunter.

Types of Odor-Control Products

Over the years, dozens of magic potions have been sold, all promising to make the hunter's odor undetectable by deer. Some of these products helped slightly, but some were outright rip-offs. As a result, many hunters became skeptical of the promises. But several new types of scent-control products are now available, and we've found them to be very effective. When used as directed, they dramatically reduce human odors, making it more difficult for deer to detect you.

Soda-based liquid sprays work by raising skin pH levels, slowing the growth of the bacteria responsible for much of our human odor. These products use either baking soda (pH 8) or washing soda (pH 12) as their active ingredient. Unfortunately, this thin film of soda can't neutralize bacterial growth forever and is soon overwhelmed. In the time it takes to walk from your truck to a hunting stand, your odor might already be detectable by a deer.

Another type of product is a *liquid oxidizer.* It combines with organic compounds, like body oils, perspiration and odor-causing bacteria, and changes them into nonvolatile salts that have no odor at all. Of course, liquid oxidizers eventually lose their effectiveness, too, but they perform considerably longer than soda-based products and can be re-applied several times during the day.

Newly available are *odor-control powders,* the best of which consist of 75 percent baking soda and 25 percent of a crystal material called Abscents®. Abscents crystals are an alumino-silicate compound with an elaborate honeycombed molecular structure that can absorb an enormous quantity of odor-producing gas molecules. With baking soda to raise skin pH and slow bacterial growth, and Abscents crystals to absorb odor, these powders can successfully control your scent long enough for you to tap a buck soundly on the shoulder, even in unfavorable winds.

Another critical product in this elaborate act of odor defiance is the Scent-Lok® suit, a garment lined with thousands of dots of activated carbon, the same

DRY clothes by hanging them outside after washing.

STORE dry clothes in a clean cooler or plastic bag.

WEAR clean coveralls for the drive to your hunting area.

DRESS while standing on a clean rubber mat.

SPRAY odor-absorbing powder into rubber boots.

PLACE hunting clothes in a cooler before driving home.

material used in shoe deodorizing pads. Like Abscents, this microscopically creviced and fissured carbon has an extensive internal surface area, and can absorb a huge amount of odor before it is saturated. The Scent-Lok can be "de-scented" and reactivated for your next outing simply by drying it on high heat in a household clothes dryer.

The only other products needed are rubber boots, a clean rubber mat, a few unscented garbage bags and a clean cooler for storage, and unscented soaps, shampoos and detergents for washing your body and clothes.

How to Practice Odor Control

Here's the drill. Wash all hunting clothes, including underwear, handkerchiefs, gloves, hats – everything you'll wear, except your Scent-Lok suit – in scent-free laundry detergent. Also wash a special coverall that you'll wear temporarily while driving to your hunting site. Don't forget your hat; humans lose a lot of perspiration through the scalp, so make sure to launder your hat. Dry this laundry outdoors in fresh air; don't contaminate it in a dryer that smells like fabric softener or antistatic sheets.

Place the dry hunting clothes in a scent-free plastic bag, cooler or rubberized canoe bag. Clean a pair of rubber boots and store them in another scentless container. (Rubber allows less foot odor to escape than does leather and can be easily washed clean.) Put the coveralls used for driving in yet another bag.

To deer, leather really stinks, so if you must carry wallets or other items made from leather, store them in heavy Zip-Loc® bags. Bows stink too, as do grunt tubes, rattling antlers and decoys; anything you touch or use should be de-scented. Spray all equipment with a liquid oxidizer and wipe it dry with a clean cloth.

On the day of your hunt, shower with scent-free hair and body soap. Dry yourself with towels that have been washed in scent-free detergent, dried outdoors, and stored in scent-free bags. (See, we told you this strategy would take dedication.) Brush your teeth with baking soda. Use no smelly mouthwashes or deodorants.

Apply an odor-control powder liberally to your sanitized body, especially areas where you tend to sweat heavily. Don your scent-free underwear and coveralls for the drive to your hunting area. Don't stop to fill your vehicle with gas, and above all, don't smoke. Avoid eating spicy foods prior to hunting, as well.

When you arrive at your hunting area, stand on a clean rubber mat, strip off the driving coveralls and jump into your clean hunting clothes. Rub a liberal

WEAR a Scent-Lok suit under the outside layer of your hunting clothes.

amount of liquid oxidizer in your hair. Now step into your Scent-Lok suit. Finally, put on your outermost layer of hunting clothes (above). Remove your boots from their bag, dust them with odor control powder and put them on. Now you're ready to go.

To avoid breaking into an odor-producing sweat, set a leisurely pace when walking to your stand. If you must hike a significant distance, you can carry your rubber mat and hunting clothes to within a few hundred yards of your stand, then cool down and do the complete deodorizing and dressing routine. Store the coveralls and boots worn for the hike in another plastic bag, and hide it.

After the hunt, reverse the procedure for the hike back to your vehicle. In warm weather, when sweating is unavoidable, partially strip and reapply these odor-eliminating products during a lull in the hunt, or when preparing for the evening hunt.

If all these precautions and rituals sound a bit silly to you, then you're probably not a candidate for this system; you'll be better off just depending on a steady breeze to carry your odor away from the deer. But if you're a totally dedicated hunter who'll do almost anything to enjoy one of those rare close encounters with a special trophy whitetail, then this method of odor control just might be your ticket to the big celebration.

For Trophies Only

Field-Judging Trophy Bucks

In order to specifically target trophy-class bucks, a hunter must able to quickly recognize a true trophy from a slightly smaller buck. Easier said than done, because fully mature bucks usually don't stand around for judging like heifers at the county fair. Some monster bucks may not expose themselves to human eyes for more than 60 seconds in their entire lives.

At the same time, he who acts hastily finds himself dragging the wrong buck out of the woods. A buck that looks wide and heavy from the front might have just a few short tines when viewed from the side.

Field-Judging Basics

The most widely accepted scoring system for white-tails is that of the Boone and Crockett Club, official record keepers for all North American big game. To be eligible for the B & C record book, bucks must be found dead or taken in fair chase by either gun or bow. The Pope and Young Club, which maintains records for animals shot with bow and arrow only, also uses the B & C scoring system.

Both clubs maintain records in typical and non-typical categories. In the *typical* category, the more closely the two antlers match, the better the net score. Under the scoring system for typicals, deductions are made for asymmetry, meaning that unbalanced racks don't score as well as perfectly balanced ones of the same general dimensions. The minimum net score for a buck to qualify as a B & C typical is 170 points; P & Y, 125 points.

Many hunters prefer the rough-and-ready character of *non-typical* racks with odd-shaped sticker points and drop tines (p. 117). As far as these sportsmen are concerned, any antler the buck manages to grow atop its head is just fine. Under the B & C scoring system, non-typical antlers are scored the same as typicals, with the usual deductions for asymmetry, but all abnormal points are then *added* to the final score. Minimum entry score for a B & C non-typical is 195 points; P & Y, 150 points.

Estimating antler size in the field is done by comparing the features of the antlers against other anatomical features of known dimension (p. 115).

For example, the ears of a mature buck are generally 6 to 8 inches long; the spread between the tips of the ears, 16 to 18 inches. The nose-to-eye distance on most mature bucks is 7 to 8 inches, and the circumference of the eye is about 4 inches.

Knowing these dimensions lets you estimate the pertinent antler measurements of the B & C scoring system: the length of the main beam and each tine; the circumference of the main beam, measured at the base and between the tines; and the inside spread between the antlers. But you'll need to do these calculations as quickly as possible; you often have little time to judge these measurements and add them for a rough estimate of the buck's score.

The best training for field-judging antlers is to study photographs and, more important, mounted heads of known score. Practice by studying mounted heads from different angles, estimating the antler measurements by comparing them to the anatomical features. Use a tape measure to check your guess.

Memorize how a 22-inch-wide rack looks from the front compared to an 18-inch rack. Notice how a long main beam reaches back, swings wide, then curls forward toward the deer's nose (right), while a shorter beam usually remains straight at the tips. If you find a set of antlers that curls in at the tips, measure them for beam length – you'll be surprised to discover these curved antlers are much longer than they first appear.

After a little practice, you'll soon develop a knack for estimating a buck's general score at a glance. That's the key for quickly and accurately field-judging live bucks.

PRACTICE your field-judging skills by attending whitetail shows. As you walk down the aisles, quickly guess the scores of the mounted bucks. After a few hours of practice, your estimates should be very close to the actual scores.

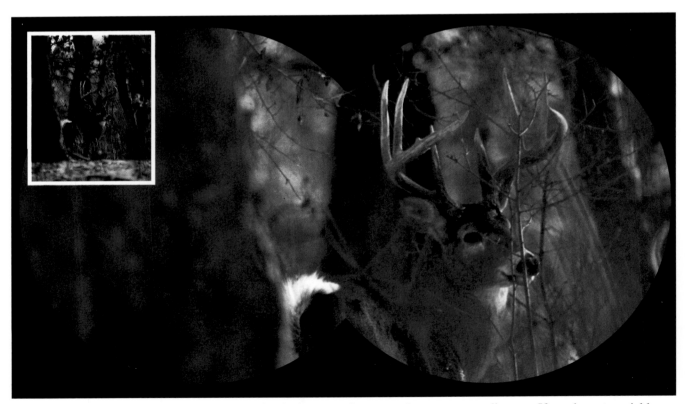

CARRY binoculars. Big bucks are secretive animals that may give you only momentary glimpses. If you learn to quickly judge rack size using binoculars, you'll be less likely to shoot the wrong buck.

LOOK at your buck's rack from several angles. Head-on (left) the buck's rack may appear to have few points, but a side view (right) could reveal many more.

WAIT until you see both antlers before deciding to shoot. Antlers may be badly asymmetrical, with tines that are deformed, missing or broken off. Sometimes an entire antler is gone.

TRAIN yourself to count points quickly. Look at one side of the rack and note how many tines project off the main beam. Don't bother to count the beam tip or brow tine, just add them later. Thus, if you see two main tines, the buck is probably an 8-pointer (left), a poor candidate for Boone & Crockett trophy status unless the rack is exceptionally large. Three tines indicate a 10-point buck (right) with much more potential for a high score.

Measuring Up

While it's relatively easy to learn how to estimate a buck's general score – for instance, a 110-class typical verses a 150 – if you're hoping to take a buck that qualifies for either record book, you'll need to learn how to score more precisely.

First, count the tines on one antler, guess the length of each and add these measurements. Now, estimate the length of the main beam, plus its circumference at the base and between the tines; add these numbers to your score. Next, double this number, assuming the other antler is relatively symmetrical to the first. Finally, estimate the inside spread between the antlers and add this number to get the total rough score. If time permits, you can subtract points for broken or missing tines. Here's an example of how you might use a quick field-scoring system:

Let's assume you're stand-hunting with a rifle and you see a deer trot through an opening in the brush. You see the rack – it's heavy, tall and wider than the distance between the tips of the ears. These features alone place it roughly in the 130- to 150-class, and if you sensed the buck was about to bolt, you might take a shot based only on this glance.

But the buck is in no hurry. He stops, presenting himself broadside, and you quickly focus his head in your binoculars. You see three tall tines sticking up from the main beam, so he's probably a 10-pointer.

You can't yet see the brow tine, but the next tine up (the G-2 tine in the scoring system) looks about 2 inches longer than the ear (which you know is about 8 inches long), making this tine close to 10 inches. The next tine is shorter, about 6 inches; the third is about half as long as the ear; call it 4 inches. Add 10,

6, and 4 for 20 points. You'll add in the length of the brow tine when the buck turns to expose it.

You see that the main beam stretches forward to halfway between the buck's eye and nose and reaches pretty high above his head. You decide that the main beam looks to be about three times longer than the 8-inch eye-to-nose distance, giving you 24 inches. Add this number to the previous score, for a total of 44.

While waiting for the buck to present a front-on view, you can score the antler mass by estimating the circumference of the main beam. The base of the antler looks considerably larger than the circumference of the buck's eye, which is about 4 inches, so you guess the antler is about 6 inches around. That's thick! The beam stays thick past the first and second points before beginning to taper off, so you add 6 plus 6 plus 5 plus 4 to arrive at 21. Added to the previous 44 points, you've now scored a total of 65. Double this score for the other antler and you're already up to 130 – and you haven't yet added in the spread between antlers or the length of the brow tines.

Finally the beast turns and looks right at you, revealing antlers that extend about 1 inch beyond the tip of each ear. You know the distance between the tips of his ears is about 18 inches, so that means the antler spread must be about 20 inches. You're up to 150 points. Now you see the brow tines; they are surprisingly short, only about 4 inches long. Double this number for 8 inches, and add this in for a total score of 158!

Do you take this buck? Although its score falls below Boone & Crockett minimums, this animal is a fantastic trophy. Ultimately, it's up to each hunter to set his own criteria for what qualifies as a "shooter."

EAR LENGTH is 6 to 8 inches. Use the ear for comparison when estimating the length of the tines and main beam.

NOSE-TO-EYE DISTANCE, usually 7 to 8 inches, can help you estimate the length of the main beam and tines.

EAR SPREAD measures 16 to 18 inches between tips. Use this distance to estimate the inside antler spread. Don't be fooled by the seemingly larger spread when a buck holds his ears back (inset).

EYE CIRCUMFERENCE is about 4 inches. Use the eye for comparison when estimating antler circumference, or *mass*, near the base and between the next three tines.

A BUCK'S APPROXIMATE AGE can influence your decision to shoot. A younger 3½-year-old buck (left) will grow a much larger rack if allowed to live another season or two. A young buck can be identified by its brown coat, delicate facial features and medium body size. A fully mature buck (right) has probably reached its trophy potential. He has a heavy body, often with a pot belly and swayed back. His block-shaped face and coat are usually grayish brown.

REGIONAL BODY-SIZE DIFFERENCES can fool a hunter. Although the antlers of the bucks shown here appear to be of different sizes, both actually are trophy-quality 150-class typicals. One animal is a 130-pound Texas buck (left), while the other is a 250-pound Canadian buck (right). Keep regional differences in mind when field-judging a buck's trophy potential.

NON-TYPICAL bucks have an appeal all their own. Whitetails often grow a few sticker points, or split brow tines, but it's a rare trophy that develops the number of large abnormal points of the buck shown above. It's difficult to accurately field-judge most non-typicals, so hunters must instead evaluate the uniqueness of the rack when deciding whether to shoot.

Hunting Mature Bucks

PENNSYLVANIA BUCKS rarely grow large racks. Heavy hunting pressure takes most bucks before they reach maturity, and poor nutrition caused by overpopulation prevents surviving bucks (above) from developing record-book antlers.

"The key to tagging a certified trophy buck, one of those heavy, old bruisers with the rocking-chair rack everybody dreams of, is to hunt where one lives," claims Toby Bridges, a dedicated muzzle-loader and trophy whitetail hunter. "That sounds obvious, but it's the ultimate reality of trophy hunting. You can have the best equipment and the best tactics in the world. You can have the sharpest eyes and be the best stalker since Daniel Boone. But if there aren't any old bucks living where you hunt, the only thing you'll get is disappointment."

Toby is right, of course. The most important part of any trophy whitetail hunt is finding an area where bucks have survived long enough to grow large antlers. Trophy bucks are almost always old bucks.

During its first 3 years of life, a male whitetail is pumping nearly all its nutrition into growing bones and body muscle. It takes a buck with extraordinary genetics, eating exceptionally nutritious forage, to produce a Boone & Crockett-size rack in less than 4 years.

Between 5½ and 7½ years of age, most bucks reach their physical peak. They are done with basic body building and can now funnel nutrients into growing antlers with thick beams and numerous, long tines. After 8 years of age, bucks begin slipping into old age; and the antlers, though still heavy, begin to loose tine length. Still, these wary survivors of many hunting seasons can be impressive trophies.

Trophy-Hunting Basics

Before setting your sights on an impossible goal, try to accurately assess the quality of bucks in your hunting area (right). The antler potential of a mature buck depends largely on nutrition, and a buck that is exceptional in one area may be just an average buck in another. In most of the Southeast, bucks rarely exceed 120 Boone & Crockett points; but in much of the Midwest, where food is plentiful and nutritious, 140-class bucks are quite common. In the Canadian prairie provinces, parts of south Texas and prime tracts of the Midwest, bucks scoring 160 points or more are a real possibility for the dedicated trophy hunter.

TEXAS BUCKS living on private ranches managed for trophy deer often sport huge racks (above). Bucks living elsewhere, however, usually have smaller antlers, due to over-hunting or to poor nutrition caused by overpopulation.

MINNESOTA BUCKS grow some of the largest antlers of all North American whitetails. Throughout much of the state, moderate hunting pressure allows bucks to live to maturity, and low deer numbers result in an abundance of high-quality food. These factors, combined with good genetics, allow these animals to reach their true trophy potential.

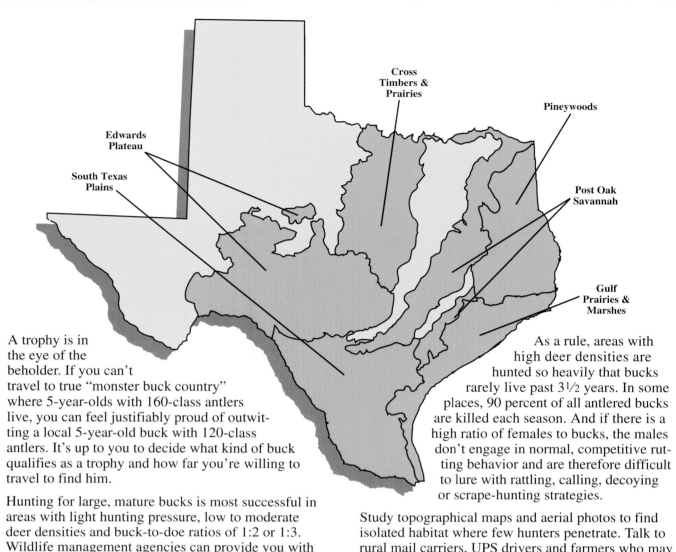

Cross Timbers & Prairies

Pineywoods

Edwards Plateau

South Texas Plains

Post Oak Savannah

Gulf Prairies & Marshes

A trophy is in the eye of the beholder. If you can't travel to true "monster buck country" where 5-year-olds with 160-class antlers live, you can feel justifiably proud of outwitting a local 5-year-old buck with 120-class antlers. It's up to you to decide what kind of buck qualifies as a trophy and how far you're willing to travel to find him.

Hunting for large, mature bucks is most successful in areas with light hunting pressure, low to moderate deer densities and buck-to-doe ratios of 1:2 or 1:3. Wildlife management agencies can provide you with these statistics (below). Don't be concerned if hunter-success statistics are low. High hunter success generally means only that large numbers of immature bucks are being taken each year.

As a rule, areas with high deer densities are hunted so heavily that bucks rarely live past 3½ years. In some places, 90 percent of all antlered bucks are killed each season. And if there is a high ratio of females to bucks, the males don't engage in normal, competitive rutting behavior and are therefore difficult to lure with rattling, calling, decoying or scrape-hunting strategies.

Study topographical maps and aerial photos to find isolated habitat where few hunters penetrate. Talk to rural mail carriers, UPS drivers and farmers who may have seen large bucks. If possible, scour the winter range after snow melt, looking for shed antlers. Drive area roads at dawn and dusk, and watch feed fields with binoculars.

Trophy Potential in Selected Regions of Texas (Based on Statistics from the 1993-1994 Hunting Season)

Ecological Areas	Number of hunters per 1,000 acres	Percentage of harvested bucks in each age class (yrs.)							
		1½	2½	3½	4½	5½	6½	7½	8½ +
Pineywoods	9.9	46.5	29.7	16.9	4.6	1.9	0.3	0.0	0.0
Gulf Prairies & Marshes	11.4	40.4	31.4	16.0	7.1	3.2	0.0	1.9	0.0
Post Oak Savannah	11.9	51.4	28.5	14.8	3.9	1.2	0.3	0.0	0.0
Cross Timbers & Prairies	13.3	50.6	20.9	17.4	7.6	2.4	0.9	0.0	0.0
South Texas Plains	6.7	22.8	12.8	20.5	13.9	13.9	11.4	3.5	1.2
Edwards Plateau	8.9	26.6	21.0	24.7	13.5	9.0	4.1	0.7	0.5

EXAMINE statistics on hunting pressure and age structure of bucks harvested when deciding where to hunt trophy whitetails. In the example above, the South Texas Plains region had only 6.7 hunters per 1,000 acres during the 1993-94 season. Of the bucks they killed, an incredible 28.8 percent were from 5½ to 7½ years of age. In comparison, the Cross Timbers and Prairies region had about twice the number of hunters per 1,000 acres, and only 3.3 percent of the bucks fell into the same age class.

Getting Permission
to Hunt on Private Land

For most hunters, the hardest part of taking a trophy buck is getting permission to hunt the land it calls home. Thousands of acres of private land in North America – small farms, huge ranches, broken suburban lots and bordering crop fields – are closed to hunting. Hundreds of bucks live within such sanctuaries, safe from human predators.

How do you find such places? Just look for the signs. *Posted. No Hunting. No Trespassing.* Listen for rumors flying around town about the huge buck seen crossing Johnson's road. Ask at the local cafe and gas station. Who's been seeing big bucks? Who got the big bucks last year? Call these folks and get friendly with them. Join the local hunting club and exchange information. If you hear about a big buck on private land, make it your goal to gain access where no one else is allowed.

Your first option is to take up the bow. Archers are often welcomed in places closed to gun hunters. Second, get to know the landowners. Don't be shy and don't let the "No" signs frighten you. Many farmers post their property just to keep from being pestered, or to cover themselves against frivolous lawsuits. If you know who owns a piece of hot property, make a phone call or drive out for a visit. If you don't know the owner, check county plat maps (p. 11) or ask around at the local co-op or farm-equipment retailer.

When you visit, be open, honest and friendly. Tell the landowner you're always looking for a beautiful, quiet place to hunt, where you can get away from the crowds and enjoy nature. Tell him you're after mature bucks only and have no interest in shooting fawns or females (unless the landowner wants you to remove a doe for management reasons). You hunt by yourself and want the challenge of hunting the smartest buck in the countryside. And offer to help a farmer with his evening chores as payment for the right to hunt his property.

If he turns you down, respect his reasons, but try to counter them tactfully if you can. Many landowners post their land because they've had bad experiences with inconsiderate hunters. Assure him you won't drop litter, start fires or leave gates open. Offer to park in his yard while you hunt, or leave him your hunting license number. Provide character references from other farmers and respected locals. If he still says no, thank the landowner as you leave, but keep his name and address in your files. Several months later, send him a Christmas card or a brief note describing your latest hunting season. Try again next year. Polite persistence sometimes wears down resistance. Another strategy is to ask permission simply to take photographs or look for antlers on the property. If a friendship or mutual respect blossoms, you can later ask for permission to hunt.

In essence, you are "courting" Mr. or Ms. farmer. If you show a genuine interest in them as people and can convey a sincere love of the outdoors and respect for their land, your chances are good for winning them over. In the end, you may find, as we have, that making new friends only improves you as a hunter.

121

TROPHY BUCKS frequently are nocturnal animals – not because they "know" that humans can't hunt at night, but rather because simple experience over several seasons has conditioned them to associate darkness with safety.

Visit local taxidermists and learn what the trophy potential is for the area. What's the usual rack size? How many record-book bucks are taken each year?

When you've discovered a suitable hunting area, begin narrowing your search using the techniques outlined in Scouting (p. 8). Your goal is to locate at least three trophy bucks so you'll have hunting opportunities throughout the season, even if someone else kills one of "your" bucks. If you actually spot the bucks, great; but it's likely you'll have to settle for second-hand evidence, such as finding large tracks or big shed antlers, or a description from an eyewitness. Try to get permission to hunt as much land as possible (p. 121). Your chances of harvesting a buck will be greatest if you have permission to hunt the land around his bedding area, because this is where he spends most of his time.

How to Hunt for Trophy Bucks

Once you've confirmed the existence of a mature buck, the hard part is over and the fun begins. Forget the old myths about superbucks. There is nothing supernatural about a trophy buck, and no reason for you to feel intimidated. A stupendous set of antlers simply means the buck is old, and the main reason

he's old is probably because hunting pressure has been light in his territory. The argument about whether an old buck is more intelligent than other deer will probably never be resolved, but one thing is certain: during the rut your buck will be susceptible to the same strategies that work with younger bucks – rattling, decoying, calling and scrape-hunting.

But there's no denying that the trophy buck is a special animal that requires a special hunter with unusual dedication, patience and restraint. For one thing, a mature trophy buck is calmer and less energetic than the young guys. Rather than dashing about and exposing himself to hunters, he's learned to lay low and watch carefully, knowing that most humans will overlook him (right). As a veteran of many seasons, he's use to

DURING THE RUT, mature bucks spend much of the day chasing females. For the trophy hunter, this is the best time to match wits with an experienced old buck.

seeing, smelling and hearing hunters at dawn and dusk, so he generally waits until night to move about.

The old buck is a creature of leisure and habit, with periodic moments of energy. He lies resting most of the daylight hours, and often chooses the shortest distances possible between food, water and bed. If he found refuge on an island during one hunting season, he'll remember to seek out the same island in following seasons. Only during the rut does the old boy rouse himself for frenzied action – this is your best chance for taking him (above).

The trophy hunter is a unique character himself, a hunter who might sacrifice three weeks' vacation each year to target a single, elusive buck. He endures cold, dark mornings, walks miles out of his way when necessary, sits on uncomfortable stands for hours, and wakes to do it all again the next day. He also has the willpower to resist smaller prey. It isn't easy holding the string or easing off the trigger when a 130-class buck stands broadside, but that's what you must do if you're waiting for a 150-class animal. To tag such a buck, you can never let him know he's being hunted. If a mature buck knows you're after him, you might as well pack it in and wait for next season.

Serious trophy hunting is a year-round commitment. The true trophy hunter is constantly honing his skills and gleaning information about his prey – visiting woods and fields, scouting, arguing biology and hunting strategy with other hunters. He's always looking for that edge.

Seasoned trophy hunters like Toby Bridges (below) know that information is power. Learn as much as possible about your quarry: Where, when and what does your buck eat?

Where does he drink? Where does he sleep, walk, rub, scrape and chase females? Where does he hide when hunting pressure gets intense? We've known hunters who take several years to piece together such a profile, but once you know your buck this well, you're ready for the most memorable hunt of your life.

Index

Cowles Creative Publishing, Inc. offers a variety of how-to books. For information write:

Cowles Creative Publishing Subscriber Books
5900 Green Oak Drive
Minnetonka, MN 55343

Books available from the publisher: *The Art of Freshwater Fishing, Cleaning & Cooking Fish, Fishing With Live Bait, Largemouth Bass, Panfish, The Art of Hunting, Fishing With Artificial Lures, Walleye, Smallmouth Bass, Dressing & Cooking Wild Game, Freshwater Gamefish of North America, Trout, Secrets of the Fishing Pros, Fishing Rivers & Streams, Fishing Tips & Tricks, Fishing Natural Lakes, White-tailed Deer, Northern Pike & Muskie, America's Favorite Fish Recipes, Fishing Man-made Lakes, The Art of Fly Tying, America's Favorite Wild Game Recipes, Advanced Bass Fishing, Upland Game Birds, North American Game Animals, North American Game Birds, Advanced Whitetail Hunting, Understanding Whitetails, Fly-Fishing Equipment & Skills, Fly Fishing for Trout in Streams–Subsurface Techniques, Fly-Tying Techniques & Patterns, Fly Rod Gamefish–The Freshwater Species, Bowhunting Equipment & Skills, Wild Turkey, Muzzleloading, Duck Hunting*

Contributing Photographers (Note: T=*Top*, C=*Center*, B=*Bottom*, L=*Left*, R=*Right*, I=*Inset*)

Charles J. Alsheimer
Bath, New York
©*Charles J. Alsheimer pp. 25TR, 32, 47CL, 47CR, 60-61, 66-67, 98, 102T, 123T*

Mike Biggs
Fort Worth, Texas
©*Mike Biggs pp. 48-49, 50T, 64*

Denver Bryan
Bozeman, Montana
©*Denver Bryan pp. 22, 38, 96-97, 115I, 123BL*

Gary Clancy
Bryon, Minnesota
©*Gary Clancy pp. 13BL, 24BR, 25BL, 27BR, 27CL, 40T, 55R, 63TL, 80, 87*

Jeanne Drake
Las Vegas, Nevada
©*Jeanne Drake pp. 92-93, 116BL*

The Green Agency
Belgrade, Montana
©*Bill Vaznis pp. 25BR, 27BL, 52BL*

Donald M. Jones
Troy, Michigan
©*Donald M. Jones pp. 16-17, 44, 53T, 57, 110, 116TR, 121*

Bill Kinney
Ridgeland, Wisconsin
©*Bill Kinney pp. 14I, 75, 81, 108-109, 113BL, 113BR, 116TL, 116BR, 119*

Lance Krueger
McAllen, Texas
©*Lance Krueger pp. 4, 8-9, 13TL, 103BR, 111, 115BL, 118B*

Bill Lea
Franklin, North Carolina
©*Bill Lea pp. 18RC, 50BR, 68-69, 74, 113TL, 113TR, 114R, 115TL, 115BR, 117, 118T, 122*

Steve Maas
Minnetonka, Minnesota
©*Steve Maas pp. 14BR, 40BR, 86T, 112B, 114L*

Bill Marchel
Fort Ripley, Minnesota
©*Bill Marchel pp. 6-7, 59, 83L, 112T*

Ted Rose
North Manchester, Indiana
©*Ted Rose pp. 58, 115TR*

Ron Spomer
Troy, Idaho
©*Ron Spomer pp. 19, 42BR*

Cooperating Manufacturers

Cabela's – World's Foremost Outfitter
812 13th Avenue
Sidney, NE 69160
1-800-237-4444

Browning
Customer Information
One Browning Place
Morgan, UT 84050

Mountaineer Archery, Inc.
P.O. Box 2208
Huntington, WV 25722